GALLOGL

For my friend Keith Durham
who first introduced me to the galloglas some ten years ago
in the outer bailey of a border fortress 'by the English called Wark'.

GALLOGLAS

*Hebridean and West Highland
Mercenary Warrior Kindreds
in Medieval Ireland*

JOHN MARSDEN

TUCKWELL PRESS

First published in Great Britain in 2003 by
Tuckwell Press Ltd
The Mill House
Phantassie
East Linton
East Lothian, Scotland

ISBN 1 86232 251 1

The publishers acknowledge subsidy from the
Scottish Arts Council towards the publication of this volume.

British Library Cataloguing-in-Publication Data
A catalogue record is available
on request from the British Library

Typeset by Hewer Text Ltd, Edinburgh
Printed and bound by Creative Print & Design, Ebbw Vale, Wales

CONTENTS

ILLUSTRATIONS

ACKNOWLEDGEMENTS

The author of any book such as this is inevitably indebted to the work of numerous others, all of whom I have sought to acknowledge in the main text or in the notes and references. There is one authority, however, who merits a more prominent acknowledgement because without the benefit of Gerard A. Hayes-McCoy's pioneering work on the galloglas these following pages would have been venturing into territory almost entirely uncharted.

In the more practical sphere of access to source material, I gratefully acknowledge the assistance of the Stornoway headquarters of Western Isles Libraries – most especially on the part of Mrs Margaret Martin – and also of Inverness Reference Library. A word of gratitude is due to my friend Michael Robson for drawing my attention to a key passage in the writing of Martin Martin, as it is also to my publisher John Tuckwell who has borne generously with this project from its very first tentative proposal.

JM

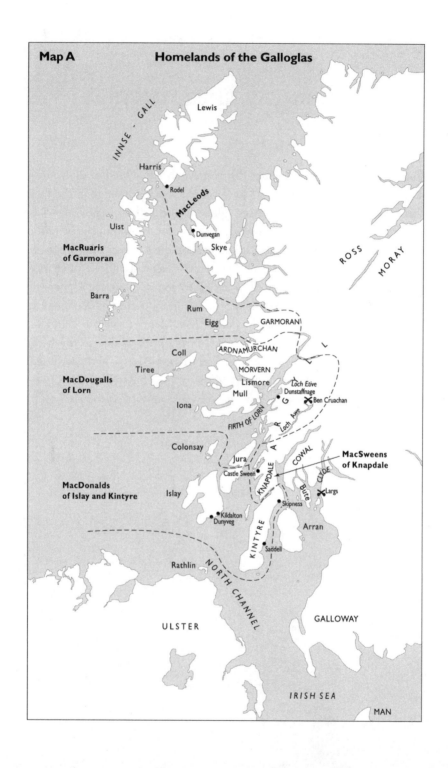

Map A **Homelands of the Galloglas**

INNSE - GALL

Lewis

Harris

Rodel

MacLeods

Uist

Dunvegan

Skye

**MacRuaris
of Garmoran**

ROSS

MORAY

Barra

Rum

Eigg

GARMORAN

Coll

ARDNAMURCHAN

L

Tiree

MORVERN

**MacDougalls
of Lorn**

Lismore

Loch Etive

Dunstaffnage

Mull

A
R
G

Ben Cruachan

Iona

Loch Awe

FIRTH OF LORN

Colonsay

A

Jura

COWAL

**MacSweens
of Knapdale**

Castle Sween

Knapdale

Bute

CLYDE

**MacDonalds
of Islay and Kintyre**

Islay

Skipness

Largs

Kildalton

Dunyveg

Arran

K
I
N
T
Y
R
E

Saddell

Rathlin

NORTH CHANNEL

ULSTER

GALLOWAY

IRISH SEA

MAN

Map B   **Ireland of the Galloglas**

NORTH CHANNEL

KINTYRE

Islay

Tory Island

Rathlin

NA TUATH   FANAD

Kilmacrenan ●

MacSweeney

Knockavoe

MacDonnell of Antrim

Farsetmore

O'Donnell of Tyrconnell

MacDonnell

U L S T E R

BANAGH

Donegal

O'Neill of Tyrone

O'Rourke

Sligo

Maguire of Fermanagh

MacMahon of Oriel

MacSweeney

Beltra Strand

B R E I F N E

MacCabe

O'Reilly

MacDonnell

MacRannell

Faughart

MacSheehy

Dundalk

MacDowell

MacWilliam Burke of Mayo

O'Connor

R O S C O M M O N

C O N N A C H T

MacSweeney

Knockdoe

Shrule

Clanricard Burke

THE ENGLISH PALE

IRISH SEA

Dublin ●

MacSheehy

MacSweeney

O'Brien of Thomond

Earldom of Kildare

MacDonnell

L E I N S T E R

Earldom of Ormond

Monasternenagh

MacSweeney

Lixnaw

Kilmallock

Fitzmaurice of Kerry

M U N S T E R

MacSheehy

MacSweeney

Earldom of Desmond

MacCarthy

Cork ●

Kinsale

PREFACE

Thinking back now over the ten years since I first learned anything of the galloglas – and at a time when I had no thought of writing a book about them – so many things come to mind which would seem to have seeded themselves there as future sources of 'inspiration'. One or two paintings by the fine military illustrator Angus McBride have long been fixed in the memory, and such time as I have spent in Ireland, although far too little, has left some sense of its landscape, accompanied by the music of its place-names, in there too. The prospect of the coastline of Antrim and Donegal seen across the North Channel from the Rhinns of Islay is always so clear in the imagination, but more haunting still are gaunt images of Gaelic warriors remembered from medieval grave-slabs throughout the West Highlands, and most especially from those in the roofless chapel at Kildalton.

In truth, though, it can only have been the preparation of my last book which somehow brought all those fragments together to inspire this new one, so there is good reason to introduce *Galloglas* as the natural successor (rather than any sort of 'sequel') to *Somerled and the emergence of Gaelic Scotland*. I have certainly come to think of it as such and not just because four of the six kindreds who form its subject were able to claim descent from the great Somerled of Argyll. The more important common ground shared by the two books lies in their reflection of my interest in the Norse component of the Celtic-Scandinavian fusion binding the deepest cultural roots of modern Gaelic Scotland. The previous book proposed Somerled as the historical figure most representative of the first fully-fledged emergence of that cultural fusion. This one will suggest the Hebridean and West Highland mercenary warrior kindreds who settled in Ireland in the thirteenth and fourteenth centuries to make so remarkable an impact on the subsequent course of medieval Irish military history as a later – if not, indeed, the last distinct – example of that same phenomenon.

It was the eminent Irish scholar and politician Eoin MacNeill who first pointed to the importance of the galloglas in his *Phases of Irish History* published over eighty years ago. Since when successive generations of Ireland's historians have had occasion to lend the subject further consideration, G. A. Hayes-McCoy outstanding amongst them but others also able to offer new insights and useful points of information even when working within wider contexts which often relegate mercenary warriors to the periphery of greater events. In their land of origin, however, the galloglas have suffered the most grievous neglect, and so much so that just ten years ago a Dublin professor was able to complain of their having been 'almost totally ignored by Scottish historians'.[1] Indeed, a similar conclusion had been reached some forty years earlier by a Scottish historian, whose concise but seriously interested article on the subject is the only such work that I have been able to find in Scottish scholarly publications, when he ruefully admitted that the galloglas 'must be considered, on this side of the Irish Sea at least, to represent a forgotten chapter of West Highland history'.[2]

If these following pages can achieve even the most modest improvement on that sad situation, then their author will be well content, but it must be said that a detailed narrative history of the galloglas would require the collaboration of a team of Irish and Scottish scholars, including amongst them specialists in medieval genealogy and military history. Such a work lies beyond the resources of a freelance writer pulling in single harness, so this book will not attempt to scale any such heights. It sets out instead to offer an introductory account of the galloglas written from the viewpoint of their original homeland on Scotland's western seaboard and in the belief that their importance for Ireland's history should not entirely obscure their significance in the story of Gaelic Scotland.

The preface to a book written in English on a Gaelic subject should include a note on the naming of names. After some thought and even at the risk of being considered inconsistent, I have decided to use the form of name which feels right to me in the historical context, just as long as it does not intimidate the reader with the more frightening excesses of medieval Irish Gaelic spelling. For example, the English form of Hugh is most familiar – and seems quite suitable – for the given name of the O'Neill earl of Tyrone at the end of the sixteenth century, while the same name in its Gaelic form of *Aodh* feels more appropriate for an O'Neill king of Ailech in the first half of the eleventh century. As a general policy, though, I have preferred to use the phonetic anglicised forms of Irish names and, wherever appropriate and helpful, to include the Gaelic – or, in other instances, the English – form in parentheses.

For the surnames of the galloglas kindreds I have used the anglicised Irish name-forms of MacSweeney, MacDonnell, MacRory and MacDowell for their members resident in Ireland, whilst retaining the Scottish forms of those names – MacSween, MacDonald, MacRuari and MacDougall – to distinguish their forebears and kinsmen in Scotland. MacSheehy and MacCabe – although applied to kindreds of originally Scottish descent – are names first occurring in Ireland and so do not present any such inconvenience.

With those necessary authorial apologia behind me, I press on in the simple hope that the reader who has survived thus far will remain sufficiently undaunted to continue in quest of these extraordinary axemen called galloglas . . .

JM

I

INTRODUCTION

'From the Western Isles . . .'

Although it seems most unlikely that the question has ever been included in any survey, my own suspicion is that the great majority of readers who know anything of the galloglas will have first come upon them by way of a passing reference in Shakespeare's *Macbeth*, so perhaps that passage from the famous play might similarly serve as a port of entry here. It occurs at the point in the first act where the ominous gloom of the three witches gives way to a martial fanfare with news brought from the battlefield to King Duncan of Scotland and his son Malcolm:

> . . . the merciless MacDonald –
> Worthy to be a rebel, for to that
> The multiplying villainies of nature
> Do swarm upon him – from the Western Isles
> Of kerns and galloglasses is supplied . . .[1]

In view of the unfortunate discrepancy between the account of events offered by the Shakespearian tragedy and the real history of eleventh-century Scotland, it is hardly surprising that even these few lines from the play contain their own quota of anachronisms.

First of all, there was no 'merciless MacDonald' at the time in which the play is set, because that kindred was descended from and named for Somerled's grandson Donald, whose death is dated to 1289 by Clan Donald tradition although more realistically placed at least twenty years earlier and thus still more than two hundred years after Duncan was slain in 1040. There were no 'kerns . . . from the Western Isles' at any time because the term is the anglicised form of the Irish *ceithearnaigh* and specifically identifies lightly-armed native mercenary infantry in medieval Ireland. Neither, and most importantly here, is there any reference to 'galloglasses' – a term which is not strictly meaningful in a Scottish context anyway – to be found anywhere until nearly two and half centuries after Macbeth's reign.

There is no record of how Shakespeare came to know of such warriors, although some galloglas had been seen in London in the early January of

1562 – when they arrived in the retinue of Shane O'Neill, the rebel lord of Tyrone who had come to negotiate with Queen Elizabeth – and there attracted the astonished attention described in the closely contemporary *Annales* of William Camden:

> And now Shane O'Neill came from Ireland, to keep the promise he had made a year before, with an escort of galloglas armed with battle-axes, bare-headed, with flowing curls, yellow shirts dyed with saffron, large sleeves, short tunics and rough cloaks, whom the English followed with as much wonderment as if they came from China or America. [2]

Shakespeare was not born until two years after the O'Neill had returned to Ireland and Camden's *Annales*, although set down in the 1590s, were not published until 1630, so it is thought most likely that the playwright learned of 'kerns and galloglasses' from English soldiers and adventurers returned from the Irish wars, who would have been frequenting London taverns in some numbers by the time he was at work on *Macbeth* in 1606. However he did come upon the term and whatever he might have understood by it, Shakespeare's reference to the galloglas is substantially historically accurate on one point at least, because these most fearsome of Ireland's fighting-men could indeed be said to have come originally 'from the Western Isles', if that term is taken to encompass the full extent of the Hebrides and their West Highland coastland.

In fact, the Gaelic origin of the word points quite precisely in that direction, because 'galloglas' (later corrupted into the double plural 'galloglasses' and the still more cumbersome 'gallowglasses') was the anglicised form of the Irish term *gallóglaigh*,[3] the plural of the noun *gallóglach* formed from *gall*, meaning 'foreign', and *óglach*, 'young man', effectively 'young warrior'. The term *gall* was most widely applied by the Irish sources to Scandinavians through the early medieval period,[4] principally those of Norse origin who first appeared as raiders at the end of the eighth century and remained as an influential presence in Ireland until the Norman seizure of their principal stronghold of Dublin in 1170. Thus 'galloglas' might be translated into modern colloquial English as 'Viking lads', and yet from the point of its first appearance in the Irish annals at the end of the thirteenth century the term is consistently associated with mercenary warrior kindreds resident in Ireland but bearing Scottish surnames of Hebridean and West Highland origin. The Scottish Gael – who were, of course, originally from Ireland and their language with them – had never been referred to as *gall* by the Irish sources, but since the extensive Norse settlement along Scotland's western seaboard in the ninth century the Hebridean archipelago had become known to the Irish as *Innse-Gall.*

These 'isles of the foreigners' continued to be so called into the fourteenth century – and thus for some time after they had been formally reclaimed from Norwegian sovereignty by the Scottish crown in 1266 – which bears testimony to Irish recognition of the enduring Scandinavian character of the culture and society of the Hebrides and, by inevitable association, of the adjacent West Highland coastland also. So, too, the *gall* component of *gallóglaigh* signifies a similar recognition of the Scandinavian aspects and associations of mercenary warriors lately arrived in Ireland across the North Channel. As the Irish military historian Gerard Hayes-McCoy pointed out in the first substantial account of the galloglas which appeared in 1937, they 'were "foreign" [i.e. *gall*] because of the Norse element in the mercenary families, not because they came to Ireland from Scotland'.[5]

That 'Norse element', however, is rather differently understood nowadays than it was in the 1930s and so, by reason of its forming such a key component of the galloglas phenomenon, the development and character of the Gaelic-Norse background from which they emerged will bear some closer consideration here.

The Scandinavian impact first came upon Ireland and the western seaboard of Scotland in the same form and at much the same time – as a sudden eruption of viking raids on island monasteries through the Hebrides and around the Irish coast in the mid-790s – but thereafter developed along quite different lines.

Evidence for the earliest Norse presence in the Outer Hebrides, although largely preserved in place-name survivals, still indicates a similar pattern to that in Orkney and Shetland with the islands having been first used as forward bases for raiding further south against the great and wealthy monasteries in Ireland itself. So too on the Irish mainland, where viking fleets first moored on loughs and coastal inlets to enable more extensive raiding inland, permanent bases became established in coastal locations, subsequently developing into miniature kingdoms which formed the foundation of Ireland's earliest towns and cities – Dublin, of course, first and foremost amongst them. For all their maritime and trading significance and their importance, even if largely as a catalyst, in Irish political history of the earlier middle ages, these 'Viking kingdoms' remained effectively self-contained Scandinavian enclaves supporting a largely transient population until they were finally dissolved into Anglo-Norman Ireland.

No such urban centres emerged in the Hebrides, where place-names confirm a more expansive settlement of farmers, who assuredly also ploughed the sea for fish and viking plunder, having followed in the wake of the first wave of sea-raiders. The same place-name evidence shows a distinct pattern of Scandinavian settlement having been most concentrated north of Skye and increasingly sparse as it extended south along the coast. In the northernmost Hebrides, where Lewis may have been entirely Norse-speaking for a time, the Norse presence has certainly obscured, and appears to have overwhelmed, whatever might have been the native cultural identity. Further south in Argyll, however, there is the least evidence of early Scandinavian settlement and, indeed, none at all around the ancient hillforts of Dunadd and Dunollie, capital strongholds of the original kingdom of the Scots. It was to Argyll (a place-name derived from the Middle Irish *Airer Gáidel* or 'coastland of the Gael') that the royal house of Dalriada in Antrim had come in the last years of the fifth century, there to place itself in kingship over earlier outposts of Irish settlement extending from the Mull of Kintyre to the Firth of Lorn. By the last quarter of the sixth century, this kingdom of 'Scotic' Dalriada had secured effective independence from Irish overkingship, but its territory – pushing further north along the seaboard even as far as Skye – would be recognised as an extension of Ireland for more than two hundred years following.

Through the eighth century the Scots of Dalriada had been greatly troubled by internecine contention and Pictish ambitions of conquest, but by the early decades of the ninth century, although seemingly untouched on the mainland by Scandinavian settlement, they were faced with the increasing Norse presence along their coastline and among their offshore island territories. The attention of their royal house had already become drawn to the east where lay the Pictish power centre of Fortriu on Tayside, and yet even as early as the 830s there is suspicion of one prominent faction in Dalriada having formed some alliance with the northmen, when a viking attack which left principal members of the Pictish royal kindred dead opened the way for Kenneth mac Alpin to seize the kingship of Dalriada and, soon afterwards, of Fortriu also.

At much the same time as the ruling house of MacAlpin moved eastward to Tayside, there to lay the foundations of the later medieval kingdom of the Scots centred on Scone, their former rivals for the kingship of Dalriada, a kindred for centuries based around the Firth of Lorn and thus more exposed to Norse pressure, had moved up the Great Glen to establish themselves on a former Pictish centre of power around the Moray Firth. So, too, when experience of repeated viking raids had driven the abbot of Iona and his monastic community to seek the greater security of Kells in the Irish midlands, Iona's eminence as the royal church of the kingdom of the Scots was conferred upon Dunkeld beside the Tay. Thus separated from church and government by the mountain chain of Drumalban (from the Gaelic *Druim Albain,* the 'dorsal ridge of Britain') dividing Perthshire from Argyll, the lesser nobility and their people left behind on the western coastland and islands of the Inner Hebrides found themselves neighbours to the northmen's great sea-road which linked Dublin to the Scandinavian homelands by way of the ship-haven in Scapa Flow. In that situation, then, they would have come into ever closer contact and to share increasing common ground with the Scandinavian presence along their coast than with the very different Picto-Scottish realm east of Drumalban.

By means of that close contact upon common ground and over not so very many generations, there came about a fusion of Norse and Gael, absorbing the Scandinavian and transforming the Celtic to create the medieval cultural province recognised by the Irish annalists as *Innse-Gall* and from which modern Gaelic Scotland is directly descended. Perhaps the most enduring symbol of that fusion is found in the maritime sphere where the West Highland galley, of such strategic bearing upon power and com-munication in the Gaelic world even into the seventeenth century, was developed from the same shipbuilding technology which had first brought the viking raiders west-over-sea. Further examples are to be found in the military sphere – as will become apparent from the history of the galloglas over a similar span of centuries – because this cultural fusion touched upon every aspect of life along the western seaboard.

It was also, and no less significantly, a fusion of bloodlines when intermarriage assuredly supplied the principal channel for cultural ex-change between northman and native, and especially so in the upper echelons of Gaelic society where marriage was a customary device to seal political alliance. Offspring of such unions are indicated by a sequence of entries in the Irish annals which make reference to warbands of viking type but identified as *Gall-Gaedhil* ('foreign [i.e. Norse] Gael'), a term first occurring in the *Annals of Ulster* at the year 856 but without any form of explanatory introduction, which can be taken as evidence for its having been already familiar in current usage by that date. None of which should be at all unexpected when the Norse had been in the Hebrides for two generations by the 850s, and neither should it be surprising that the Irish should recognise these people of mixed blood as Gael. There is, in fact, every likelihood of their having been Gaelic speakers by the mid-ninth century because it was widely characteristic of the Scandinavian expansion – and certainly in Frankish Normandy and Slavic Russia at much the same period – to very swiftly adopt the tongue of the dominant host culture. The Gaelic language, originally brought to Scotland by the Irish settlers even as early as the third century AD, would certainly have been spoken throughout the territory of Scotic Dalriada and thus as far north as Skye, but there is no evidence for its extensive penetration further north through the Hebrides before the arrival of the northmen. Thus it would follow that Gaelic did not achieve its dominance in the Outer Hebrides until after their Scandinavian settlement and probably no earlier than the last quarter of the eleventh century, by which time the full extent of the Hebridean archipelago lay within the vast sea-kingdom of Man and the Isles.

The surviving historical evidence for overlordship of the Innse-Gall in the ninth and tenth centuries is never better than fragmentary, which can probably be taken as an accurate reflection of the true state of government in the region through most of that period. The first historical personality attributed any such lordship is entered in the *Annals of the Four Masters* at 836 where he appears as an ally of Kenneth mac Alpin, and again at 853 when his obituary styles him *tóisech* ('chieftain of') *Innsi Gall*, the form of his name in both entries being of especial significance because *Gofraidh mac Fearghus* ('Gothfrith, son of Fergus') indicates him as the son of a Norse mother and Gaelic father. Through the following two hundred and fifty years such evidence as is preserved across a range of Irish, Scottish and Scandinavian sources indicates intermittent lordship of the Hebrides having been passed between the Norse power-centres of Dublin, Orkney and the Isle of Man, which had become established by the tenth century as a convenient retreat for Norse warlords expelled from Dublin.

The creation of a kingdom of the Isles centred on Man can be accredited to Godred Crovan, an adventurer traditionally associated with the Isle of Islay and yet probably descended from Norse kings of Dublin, who seized the kingship of the Isle of Man in 1079. His descendants ruled for almost two hundred years as sub-kings of the Norwegian crown, Magnus Bareleg, king of Norway, having brought a great fleet west-over-sea in 1098 to secure formal sovereignty over the Isles by agreement with the King of Scots. Within some fifty years of 1098, however, there is decisive evidence for a new Gaelic-Norse aristocracy having emerged in the old Dalriadic heartland of Argyll and Kintyre. At its head there stood the formidable figure of Somerled of Argyll – a direct descendant of Gothfrith mac Fergus and *gall-gaedhil* in his every aspect – whose galleys fought the fleet of Godred Crovan's grandson through the night around the Feast of Epiphany in the year 1156. When peace was made on the morning after the battle, Somerled had won the Inner Hebrides from the king of Man and thus laid the first foundation of his own descendants' Lordship of the Isles.

All of which has the most immediate bearing on the earliest Irish annal entries indicating the presence of galloglas in Ireland, because the three kindreds named by the annalists can be traced back to that Gaelic-Norse aristocracy of Argyll and Kintyre, and two of them back to grandsons of Somerled himself.

The very first appearance of the term 'galloglas' anywhere in the historical record occurs in an entry found in the *Annals of Connacht* and the *Annals of Loch Cé* at the year 1290 and concerning a dispute between half-brothers over succession to the kingship of Tyrconnell, Donal Og O'Donnell having been succeeded on his death in 1281 by his elder son Aodh who was later challenged by Turlough, the son borne by Donal Og's second wife:

> Aodh O'Donnell was deposed by his own brother, Turlough, who assumed the kingship himself through the power of his mother's kin, the Clan Donald, and of many other galloglas.

The annalists' casual reference to galloglas (in the Irish form of *galloclaech*) without any form of introduction, comment or explanation is so distinctly alike to the way in which the *gall-gaedhil* first appeared in the annal record of the ninth century as to lead to a similar conclusion: that fighting-men from the Hebrides and West Highlands, although unknown under that name in the annals until 1290, must have been a familiar presence in the north of Ireland for some time before that date.

Interestingly, the two wives of Donal Og were both daughters of families destined to become the two most prominent of the galloglas kindreds. While Turlough's mother was known to the annalist as the daughter of 'MacDonald of the Isles' – presumably Angus Mor, the son of Somerled's grandson Donald for whom the Clan Donald is named – the O'Clery genealogies identify his elder half-brother as 'the son of a daughter of the Mac Suibhne' and thus confirm Donal Og's first wife having been born into another kindred at that time associated with Scotland but soon to emerge as a galloglas dynasty in Ireland. A sixteenth-century history of the *Clann Suibhne* identifies her as *Caieriona* (Catriona) and her father Eoin as the nephew of the first of the name MacSweeney to be entered in the Irish annals.[6] This was the Murrough (*Murchadh*) MacSweeney who is noticed by the *Annals of the Four Masters* at 1267 when he was taken prisoner in the Owles in Mayo by a son of the O'Connor 'who delivered him up to the Earl [of Ulster] in whose prison he died'. Although the annalist makes no specific reference to Murrough MacSweeney as a galloglach, there is at least the implication of his having been active in some capacity as a warrior, but more important is the decisive evidence for the MacSweeneys – formerly associated with Knapdale on Kintyre and called the MacSweens in Scotland – having been present in Ireland by the third quarter of the thirteenth century.

Still earlier than those two annal entries is another bearing on a third galloglas kindred and found in the *Annals of Connacht* at 1259, but more fully in the *Annals of Loch Cé* at the same year where it tells of Aodh O'Connor, future king of Connacht, collecting his Scottish bride and with her a dowry of especial significance here:

> Aodh O'Connor went to Derry to marry the daughter of Dugall (*Dubhgall*) MacSomhairle, and eight score warriors came with her, and Alan (*Ailín*) Mac Somhairle with them.

That significance is clarified when the Dugall and Alan 'MacSomhairle' were, in fact, the sons of Ruari (a grandson of Somerled, hence the annalist's 'MacSomhairle'), eponym of the MacRuari kindred whose territory lay in Garmoran north of Ardnamurchan. The warriors – called *oclaech* in the annalist's original Irish – brought to Derry by Alan, uncle of the bride, can thus be considered the first recorded arrivals in Ireland of the MacRory galloglas (although unnoticed as such in the annal record until more than fifty years later).[7]

There is clear evidence, then, for representatives of three of the six galloglas kindreds having been resident in Ireland before the end of the thirteenth century, while the others make their first appearances in the annals at intervals through the following ninety years, the latest of them being the MacDowells – a branch of the MacDougalls of Lorn named for

Somerled's eldest son – who are first noticed at 1377. Ten years earlier are found the MacSheehys – another branch of descent from the Clan Donald – at 1367, and almost a decade earlier still, at the year 1358, is entered the first reference to the MacCabes, the most enigmatic of the galloglas kindreds as to their origin and yet the one with perhaps the strongest claim of all to having come 'from the Western Isles'.[8]

The dates of these first appearances in the annal record cannot be read as the most precise indication of the date of arrival of these last three kindreds in Ireland, because it is more than likely and, in some cases, quite certain – for reasons which will become apparent later – that they had arrived from Scotland even decades before the annalist had occasion to notice their activities. What can be said with every confidence is that fighting-men from the six galloglas kindreds had been finding their way to Ireland from the Hebrides and West Highlands since the middle of the thirteenth century and had become established there as professional mercenary warriors by the second half of the century following. That same period was one marked by dramatic and turbulent change in Scotland, not least in Argyll and the Isles, which must have had some bearing on the migration of these kindreds from their homeland. So it was in Ireland also, but there the galloglas were to have their own key part to play in the Gaelic resurgence which was to roll back the Norman ascendancy. It might be helpful, then, to sketch in at this point some outline of the Scottish and Irish history which forms the context for the emergence of the galloglas.

There is nowhere any record of the precise extent of the Hebrides ceded to Somerled after the Epiphany battle of 1156, and there is every likelihood that the claim made by the *Chronicle of Man* that 'this was the cause of the ruin of the kingdom of the Isles, beginning from the time when the sons of Somerled took it' was made with some benefit of hindsight. The Manx chronicler was writing more than a century after the event, by which time the sea-kingdom bequeathed by Godred Crovan to his successors had been reduced to the two islands of Lewis and Skye – in addition, of course, to the Isle of Man itself.

The 'sons' – or, by that time, the grandsons – of Somerled held lordship not only over the Islay and Mull island groups, but almost certainly also over Rum, Eigg, Barra, the Uists and possibly even south Harris as well, each of those three offshore territories pertaining to a corresponding lordship on the mainland. The Mull group lay within the lordship of

Lorn (anciently styled *Ergadia* or 'Argyll') inherited from Somerled by his eldest son Dugall and thereafter the heartland of the MacDougalls. To their south the lordship of Islay, including with it the mainland peninsula of Kintyre, had passed to Somerled's grandson Donald and thus became the power centre of his successor MacDonald Lords of the Isles, while the northernmost mainland territory of Garmoran, with the isles from Eigg to the Uists, had become the territory of the MacRuaris descended from Donald's brother, Ruari.[9]

Thus the descendants of Somerled found themselves – at least formally – sub-kings of two separate sovereignties, that of Norway for their island possessions and that of the kingdom of Scots for their mainland territories. Such a political situation in so remote a location allowed them to play off one overlord against the other or disregard both, but the westward direction taken by Scottish royal ambition even as early as the 1220s boded dramatic changes for the Gaelic-Norse magnates of the west.

The character of the kingdom of the Scots had already undergone its own great transformation as the eleventh century passed into the twelfth, and it was one starkly reflected in its attitude to the original Gaelic heartland in the west. The direct male line of descent in the house of MacAlpin had come to an end with the death of Malcolm II in 1034, when the succession passed to Malcolm's daughter's son Duncan who was brought down six years later by Macbeth, mormaer of Moray and probably also a grandson of Malcolm II with no less a claim on the kingship he was to hold for seventeen years. On their father's death, the two sons of Duncan had fled into exile, Donald to the west and Malcolm into England from where he was to return to reclaim the kingship, slaying Macbeth in 1057 and his stepson and successor Lulach in the spring of the following year.

It has been said more than once – and with some justice – that the downfall of Macbeth marked the end of the 'Celtic' kingdom of the Scots, because it was Malcolm III (more usually called Malcolm Canmore) with his English queen Margaret who provided the first foothold in Scotland for the Anglo-Norman influences which were to bring about the 'feudalisation' of the kingdom through the reigns of their descendant successor kings of the Canmore dynasty. On the death of Malcolm in 1093, however, the kingship of Scots was claimed by his brother Donald (or *Domnall Bán*, his Gaelic name-form reflecting his long years of exile in the west) who was twice driven from the kingship by the sons of Malcolm and finally deposed in 1097. The great thrust of support for *Domnall Bán* assuredly came from

Argyll and the Isles, so the claim made by the *Anglo-Saxon Chronicle* that his supporters 'drove out all the English who had been with King Malcolm before' can be taken as the first evidence of Gaeldom's antipathy to the Anglo-Norman inclination of the Canmore kings of Scots.

If the Gaelic west had become estranged from the MacAlpin kings, it was to develop open hostility to the house of Canmore throughout the twelfth century and into the first decades of the century following. Each succession of Malcolm Canmore's sons and grandsons to the kingship prompted an almost customary challenge from rival claimants claiming descent from Macbeth's short-lived successor Lulach. When each of these risings won support from the Gaelic-Norse west, it is hardly surprising that the house of Canmore came to recognise the West Highlands and the Hebrides as a spawning ground of subversion and revolt. While each outbreak of rebellion appears to have been efficiently suppressed, the attention of kings of Scots was too regularly focused on the shifting sands of their dealings with England to assert any real sovereign authority over the western outlands, their only threatening gesture in that direction being the encouragement of a Stewart fiefdom centred around Renfrew to serve as a feudal bulwark against Argyll.

It would seem to have been the period of peaceful stability in Anglo-Scottish relations in the first decades of the thirteenth century – accompanied also by access to a realistic naval capability – which enabled Alexander II to turn his attention to the west. Probably provoked by western support for the usual Moray-connected rising on his succession in 1214, Alexander launched at least one campaign around the Clyde, Cowal and Kintyre in 1221–2 as a demonstration of his intent to exert sovereignty over Argyll. The implications for the Hebrides of his new policy evidently gave cause for concern to Somerled's descendant successors, and two years later Hebridean emissaries were in Norway with an appeal to King Hakon. If preoccupations at home distracted the Norwegian king from immediate intervention, successive events were to force his hand, not least a civil war between contending royal factions on Man which erupted in 1228 and spilled out into the Isles. *Hakon's Saga* tells of his learning of this 'great dispeace west over sea' and despatch of a fleet to the Hebrides in 1230 to instal one Uspak – thought to have been a son of Dugall of Argyll settled in Norway – as his king over the Isles. The expedition found uneasy allies among Dugall's other sons in the Hebrides, but in the event came to nothing, bringing Uspak only fatal injury at the siege of Rothesay castle on Bute and a tomb in the ancient royal burial-ground on Iona.

Meanwhile Alexander of Scotland was himself distracted from westward ambitions by a new turbulence in Anglo-Scottish relations, and it was not until 1244 that he opened diplomatic approaches to purchase the Hebrides from Norwegian sovereignty. Not only were those overtures summarily rejected by Hakon, but the year 1248 found Ewen MacDougall and Dugall MacRuari in Bergen, apparently contending for the kingship which had been intended for Uspak eighteen years before. Instead, Hakon gave his daughter in marriage to Harald of Man, which would have set the traditional marital seal on Norwegian sovereignty over the Manx kingdom of the Isles had not Harald and his bride perished on voyage home when their ship went down in the Sumburgh Roosts off the southern tip of Shetland. Hakon's response to the tragedy was to send Ewen of Lorn away home with a commission to assume kingship over the Isles – and it was that which apparently provoked Ewen's Scottish sovereign to launch his expedition into the MacDougall heartland in 1249 with the intention of bringing Ewen to heel. In the event, Alexander fell suddenly ill and died on board ship in the sound of Kerrera, the campaign was abandoned and the Scottish crown's ambitions in the west put into abeyance through the twelve-year minority of Alexander's successor, his young son and namesake who was inaugurated as Alexander III within days of his father's death.

It was the reign of this third Alexander which would see the Hebrides at last restored to the kingdom of the Scots, and renewed diplomatic approaches to Norway were being made soon after the young king attained his majority in 1261. Hakon's resistance, however, remained as determined as before, and indeed rather more so when he was prepared to lead a great fleet west-over-sea to demonstrate that determination. The course of events in that last Norse royal cruise of 1263 has been worked over countless times and can be fairly swiftly summarised here. Hakon did bring a fleet down through the Hebrides in fair imitation of Magnus Bareleg's enterprise of 1098, and with much the same purpose although with quite the opposite ultimate outcome. Manx and Hebridean subject rulers were called to his aid, Ewen MacDougall refusing support (having switched his allegiance to the Scottish camp) and the others, who responded only with reluctance under pressure, being despatched over the Arrochar portage to Loch Lomond on a plunder raid which bore a striking similarity to a loyalty test. Meanwhile the Norwegian fleet sailed south for the Firth of Clyde where the weather on the west coast in the equinoctial season might be said to have done the expedition its greatest injury in driving ships ashore on the

Cumbraes and at Largs on the southern shore, a Scots force attacking beached vessels and engaging a landing party in some degree of conflict. Almost all serious modern historians have cast various measures of doubt on the significance of this 'Battle' of Largs and it certainly bore no comparison at all to the crushing defeat of Harald Hardradi at Stamford Bridge almost exactly two hundred years before. Nonetheless, the Scottish realm did display an unmistakable capacity for self-defence, the Norse did withdraw – even if under greatest pressure from the need to get home before the onset of the North Atlantic winter – and they were never to return. Putting in to Orkney on voyage home and detained there by unfavourable weather, old Hakon was taken ill and died. His son and successor Magnus was so much more amenable to negotiation that the cession of the Isles to the Scottish kingdom was formalised under the terms of the Treaty of Perth three years later.

As R. Andrew McDonald concludes in his history of the kingdom of the Isles: 'Alexander III's reign seemed to extinguish the old order in the west . . . the descendants of Somerled – the MacDougalls, MacDonalds, and others – had been forced to resolve their dilemma of divided allegiances and were, for the most part, drawn into the wider community of the realm of Scotland, which was centred on the royal court itself'.[10] He points also to a distinct reflection of that new orientation of western magnates towards the Scottish court in the choice of the name Alexander for the first-born sons of both Ewen MacDougall and Angus Mor MacDonald, because that name – quite unknown in Gaelic genealogies before the thirteenth century – does seem to be a token of homage to the king. No less significant, though, is the evidence from Clan Donald tradition for the use of the Scottish Gaelic form of *Alasdair* for the name Alexander,[11] a detail bearing its own testimony to the Gaelic aristocracy of the west having retained its own language and culture (even if only on its home turf) rather than adopting the sub-Norman French speech and style which had been characteristic of Scottish court circles since the twelfth century. Nonetheless, the political – if not cultural and linguistic – transformation of Gaelic-Norse lords of the west into barons of the realm of Scotland within a single generation is vividly illustrated by the comparison of Angus Mor, named by the saga-maker as one of the leaders of the raid across the Arrochar portage at the behest of Hakon in 1263, with his second son and successor Angus Og, who was hailed by John Barbour as the staunch ally of the Bruce in his time of peril and on his day of triumph on the field of Bannockburn.

In 1289 Alexander III took a fall from his horse after being separated from his guides riding through the night to Kinghorn, and his body was found on the Fife shore the next morning. He left no surviving heir and the realm was plunged into a crisis of succession attended by English ambitions of overlordship and leading to the Scottish Wars of Independence. Out of all of which emerged the ascendancy of the house of Bruce in the person of the first King Robert of Scotland, and with it a watershed in the fortunes of Somerled's descendant kindreds, not least the MacDonalds of Islay and the MacDougalls of Lorn who had already been long at odds with each other.

The single most decisive event for the MacDougalls was the killing by Robert the Bruce of his rival John Comyn at Greyfriars church in Dumfries in 1306, because Comyn's daughter was the wife of Ewen MacDougall's son Alexander. Thereafter the MacDougalls became most bitter and dangerous foes to the Bruce, until his crushing defeat of the forces of Alexander's son John on the slopes of Ben Cruachan in 1308 set in process the downfall of the house of Lorn. The MacRuaris and – still more importantly – eventually also the MacDonalds came out in full support of the Bruce cause, and a debt of gratitude to Angus Og was to lay the foundation for the new eminence of his descendants in the west where Angus' son John of Islay was to become the first formally-styled Lord of the Isles (*dominus insularum*) in a charter of 1354.

The ascendancy of Robert the Bruce – whose family name *de Brus*, originally *de Brieux*, derived from their ancestral lands of Brix in Normandy – could very well be said to represent the ultimate achievement of the 'Norman Conquest' of Scotland. All the more ironic, then, was his brother Edward's bid for the kingship of Ireland and the three-year military campaign in its support which made so crucial a contribution to the demolition of the Norman achievement in that country.

The Norman impacts upon Scotland and Ireland took very different forms, and both of them, of course, were quite unlike the decisive invasion of 1066 which placed Duke William of Normandy in kingship over England. In Scotland the 'feudalisation' of the kingdom had come about at the invitation of three generations of the house of Canmore and by means of its obligations to English kings, intermarriage with English royal and noble families, and the granting of Scottish estates to an Anglo-Norman aristocracy imported from the south. The first Normans arrived in Ireland also by invitation, although not that of the royal house because –

unlike Scotland – twelfth-century Ireland had no established ruling dynasty, nor was there any approximation of an 'Irish realm'. Which is not to say there were no kings in Ireland because there would seem to have been always an abundance of tribal and regional rulers bearing various ranks of that title (in forms of the Gaelic term *rí*) since the earliest historical period. By the eve of the Norman impact, when this term *rí* had come to signify a provincial king ruling his *tír* (or 'country') with lordship over his vassal chieftains, some prospect of a realistic national kingship was already coming into view.

There are claims in various sources since the seventh century for individuals having been high-kings (or *ard rí*) over all Ireland, usually in the form of 'king of Tara' and most of them scions of the Ui Neill dynasty,[12] but modern historians have recognised the first emergence of a kingship of all Ireland in the achievement of Brian Boru (from the Gaelic *bóruma*, 'of the tributes') in the first years of the eleventh century. Much as Brian emerged out of Munster to supplant the Ui Neill in the kingship of Tara in 1002, so Rory O'Connor, king of Connacht, seized the kingship of Hiberno-Norse Dublin in 1166 and might have thus created an urban capital for a unified Irish kingdom had he not, in so doing, provoked the local Leinster king Dermot MacMurrough to bring his Norman allies into Ireland.

When he resisted Rory O'Connor, Dermot was defeated and driven out, finding his way across the Irish Sea to Wales and there recruiting the Norman military support which enabled him to reclaim his kingdom soon after returning to Ireland in 1167. These, however, were just the first contingent of Dermot's Norman allies and a second – including Maurice, the first of the Fitzgeralds – arrived in 1169 bringing with it something more than five hundred fighting-men. In the following year, and with his own formidable army, there came Richard fitz Gilbert de Clare – better remembered under his cognomen of 'Strongbow' – who had been deprived of his earldom of Pembroke by Henry II, but to whom Dermot was to give his daughter as wife. With Strongbow as his ally and an Irish-Norman army at his back, Dermot was able to mount his greatest challenge to the high-kingship of Rory O'Connor – and, indeed, to shape the future history of Ireland – in September 1170 when he recaptured Dublin.

There was nothing unusual in twelfth-century Ireland about kings hiring mercenary allies, which is really all that these Normans first appeared to be, but Dermot's death in 1171 created a quite different situation when Strongbow, as his son-in-law, was able to claim for himself the kingship of Leinster. The prospect of a dissident Norman knight established as an independent ruler across the Irish Sea and within reach of reclaiming the earldom of Pembroke prompted Henry of England to mount his own expedition to Ireland with the purpose of forestalling such an eventuality on the part of Strongbow and his like. Irish kings immediately submitted to Henry, probably in the hope that his overlordship would restrain further aggressive expansion of the Norman presence, in so doing effectively gifting high-kingship of Ireland to the English crown. Rory O'Connor was not one of those who submitted in 1171, but was to do so four years later under the Treaty of Windsor which confirmed him in his own kingship of Connacht, and lordship over the rest of Ireland on payment of tribute to Henry, who reserved to himself Meath and Leinster and with them also the towns of Dublin, Wexford and Waterford. Through the following half-century, however, the treaty was to prove no obstacle to the Anglo-Norman barons who extended themselves from Leinster across Meath and Louth, into much of Munster and along the east coast of Ulster, raising castles to demonstrate their dominion over lands which they planted with peasant colonists from their English and Welsh estates.

Of necessity an absentee sovereign, Henry appointed an Anglo-Norman 'justiciar' to rule as his representative in the royal demesne lands with control of Meath from the Shannon to the Irish Sea, which – as the historian Katharine Simms has explained – effectively 'split Gaelic Ireland into two halves', allowing the English king and his justiciar the freedom of movement and military strength necessary to play the part of high-king in Ireland.[13] When Henry's youngest son John came to the English throne he appeared in Ireland still more impressively as a high-king, especially on his second visit in 1210 when he is said to have taken the submission of twenty Irish kings, including amongst them the O'Brien, O'Connor and O'Neill who apparently brought forces in his support against the recalcitrant de Lacey earl of Ulster. Yet the *Annals of Inisfallen* insist that the O'Neill merely paid his respects to the king and refused to give hostages, so it may have been that 'submission' was seen as merely a form of 'alliance' by the magnates of Gaelic Ireland.

Even so, John's reign ushered in a second wave of expansion through the thirteenth century in the form of westward migration by descendants of earlier Anglo-Norman invaders, notably the de Burghs (later anglicised to 'Burkes') into Connacht and Ulster, the Fitzgeralds into Desmond, the de Clares into Thomond and the Butlers into Ormond.[14] Much of the west of Ireland thus passed into Anglo-Norman overlordship, although not so thoroughly colonised by English and Welsh peasantry as the east and thus making the barons more extensively reliant upon native Irish tenants. They did, however, take hostages and tribute from Irish vassal kings, manipulated their succession and summoned them with all their forces to join their overlords' hostings, thus increasingly restricting the dominion of the native Gaelic rulers (now more realistically styled 'lords' than 'kings').

By the last decade of the thirteenth century every native Irish chieftain could be claimed as the vassal of a feudal overlord and the Anglo-Norman conquest had reached its greatest extent. Even by that date, however, there is already evidence of the tide turning towards a Gaelic resurgence whereby most Irish lords would free themselves from the control of the English king and his administration in Ireland. The term 'resurgence' – or sometimes 'revival' – is used by historians in preference to 'reconquest', because the gains won by the Gaelic lords were political and cultural rather than territorial, reclaiming their own independence from English overlordship, taking back the submission of their own vassal chieftains (known in the fourteenth century as 'urraghts' – from the Irish *oireacht*) and restoring their traditional customs, most significantly those associated with the ancient rituals of inauguration into kingship.

Similarly the descendants of the original invaders – themselves having been hardly the most submissive of nobility – who had pushed the Anglo-Norman expansion so far into the north and west had increasingly asserted their independence through the thirteenth century and especially in the century following when the Statute of Kilkenny of 1366 supplies the first formal evidence of their 'gaelicisation'. Its provisions insisting on the use of the English language – especially for personal names – and customs whilst prohibiting intermarriage, concubinage and fosterage with the Irish confirm the urgent concern of the administration to restrict 'contamination' of the English colony by the Gaelic resurgence. If such a risk was of official concern so near to Dublin, then it must have been still more apparent and advanced in Connacht and Munster where the descendants of the Anglo-Norman invaders would eventually be recognised as 'more Irish than the Irish'.

In fact, the first 'Anglo-Norman' invaders had come not from England but from Wales (therefore perhaps more accurately described as 'Cambro-Normans') and would have been Flemish, Norman or Welsh speakers urgently in need of some familiarity with the Gaelic language to communicate with their Irish allies, tenants and fighting-men. More thorough 'gaelicisation' came about by the most natural process within a generation or two when the sons of the first invaders took Irish wives. Thomas fitz Maurice, son of the first of the Fitzgeralds who came to Ireland in 1169 and ancestor of the earls of Desmond, whose wife had the Gaelic name *Sadhbh*, supplies just one prominent example of a widespread trend. Already by the third generation, then, prominent kindreds of Ireland's Anglo-Normans were already of mixed blood, some number of them the offspring of less formal liaisons with Irish women. As the eminent historian of Gaelic Ireland Kenneth Nicholls explains, 'children of such unions, although members by birth of a great Norman lineage and privileged as such, would have been brought up by their mothers in a purely Gaelic milieu'. He points to Sir William Liath de Burgo (d. 1324), cousin to the Earl of Ulster but the son of an O'Connor mother and husband to an O'Brien wife, as an example of a man who would have been equally at home in both worlds and whose descendants – in the political circumstances of the time – 'would pass over entirely to the Gaelic one'.[15]

The political circumstances of the time were, of course, those of the Gaelic resurgence which made such progress – in the judgement of Eoin MacNeill – that 'within a few centuries of the Norman invasion, the authority of the kings of England had shrunk to within a day's ride of Dublin and the outskirts of a few other towns'.[16] Professor MacNeill found the beginnings of this resurgence in the mid-thirteenth century when Brian O'Neill, who had withheld tribute due to the earl of Ulster in 1253, launched a campaign of raids on County Down until he was slain in battle in 1260. More recent historical opinion places its starting-point some few decades later when the revolts by the Irish of Leinster from 1271 and into the 1290s threatened the core territory of the English settlement around its administrative capital of Dublin (the region later known as the 'English Pale').

By which time the strain placed upon the English administration by its masters in London on the one hand and assertive barons with their own private armies on the other was beginning to tell. In fact, the success of the Gaelic resurgence is thought to have owed as much to this internal weakening of the English administration as it did to Irish military activity, especially when much of the fiercest conflict was between the Irish themselves as native lords fought to reclaim the submission of their former vassal chieftains. Natural forces also played their part in the erosion of the English colony, when cereal famines caused by extremely bad weather between the mid-1290s and early 1330s bore especially grievously upon the farmland of Leinster, and the Black Death which broke out in Ireland in 1348 ravaged the populations of Dublin and other towns while sparing the more numerous Irish scattered across the wilder country in the Gaelic outlands.

What can be said with every confidence of the progress of Ireland's Gaelic resurgence is that it achieved its full momentum through the first half of the fourteenth century, pointing perhaps to the inauguration of Felim O'Connor into kingship – 'in the manner remembered by the old men and recorded in the old books' according to the *Annals of Connacht* at 1310 – as a signal event of the cultural revival and a reflection of the political recovery of Gaelic Ireland. Just five years later Edward Bruce, recently appointed heir presumptive to his brother's kingship of Scots, landed with a Scottish army at Larne where he was joined by a number of Irish chieftains, the most powerful of the O'Neills foremost amongst them, who proclaimed him king of Ireland.

Throughout the three years following Edward's arrival in May 1315 it seemed that no force could withstand the Bruce invasion. He marched south to burn Dundalk, and an army led against him by Richard de Burgh, the Red Earl of Ulster, was decisively defeated at Connor in Antrim as was another led by Roger de Mortimer, lord of the great Norman castle at Trim, when Bruce marched into Meath and a specially assembled Anglo-Irish host failed to prevent his southward advance into Laois and Offaly. When that progress was hampered by the effects of famine, Edward withdrew into Ulster where Carrickfergus castle surrendered to him after months of siege. Before Christmas his brother King Robert had joined him with reinforcements from Scotland and their forces marched south in the first weeks of 1317, forcing the earl of Ulster to retreat before them and advancing towards a panic-stricken Dublin, which could have been their next objective had it not been for a disinclination to risk a lengthy siege against urgently and heavily fortified city walls. By April they were in Munster, seemingly attempting the circuit of Ireland traditionally required of a high-king, but soon afterwards Robert had returned to Scotland and Edward withdrawn to Ulster from where he was not to reappear for some eighteen months. When he did march out again in the autumn of the following year, it was to his death in battle with John de Bermingham's forces at Faughart just north of Dundalk.

The immediately realistic objective of the Bruce invasion in the year following the triumph at Bannockburn was probably to deprive Edward II of reinforcement from Ireland, but the *Annals of Connacht* suggest a greater purpose, at least on the part of King Robert himself when he arrived in 1316 'to help his brother and to expel the Gaill [i.e. the English 'foreigners'] from Ireland'. Some modern historians have taken the view that Robert may very well have had conquest of Ireland in mind and with it the hope of a Welsh alliance so that 'a great pan-Celtic invasion of England might result'.[17] Such a grand strategy would not have been uncharacteristic of the Bruce at the high peak of his ascendancy because, for all his noble Norman descent, he had been raised in Gaelic-speaking Carrick and had written of the Scots and Irish as 'our nation . . . able to recover her ancient liberty'.

It was, of course, not to be. The Bruce invasion ended in defeat at Faughart, and Edward's ambitions on kingship of Ireland were extinguished by his death in battle, so it would be reasonable to judge the whole extraordinary enterprise as having been a failure. On the other hand, Edward was able to sustain an effective occupation of Ulster for fully three years, even setting up his own administration there and arguably presaging the extinction of the de Burgh earldom in that province some fifteen years later. In fact, the Bruce intervention in Ireland can be seen now as marking an important stage in the Gaelic resurgence, and not least in its impressive demonstration to Irish chieftains that the Norman military might which had intimidated them for a century and a half could be beaten and, still more importantly here, beaten in open battle by the forces of their fellow Gael.

Before the end of the eleventh century, the Normans had proved their supremacy in arms from the sands of Hastings to the walls of Jerusalem, and so too in twelfth-century Ireland where native fighting-men, best equipped for and accustomed to cattle-raid and skirmish, were inevitably overwhelmed on the battlefield by mounted knights, mailed men-at-arms and disciplined archers. Set against that background, the impact of the Bruce invasion becomes immediately apparent, because the forces led by Edward in 1315 were battle-hardened Scottish troops – assuredly including veterans, like himself, of the victory at Bannockburn – who consistently inflicted defeat upon armies brought against them by the greatest Anglo-Norman barons of Ireland. The arrival of the reinforcements brought to Ireland by King Robert at the end of 1316 must have been ample recompense for the losses suffered in the earlier months of campaigning through a famine-stricken land, because the army led out by the Bruce brothers in 1317 was so formidable as to inspire utter panic in Dublin and to deter the English justiciar (who had a thousand troops of his own in addition to those of his loyal Anglo-Norman barons) from meeting it in battle. Whatever was the true cause of Edward's final defeat at Faughart, it has been convincingly suggested that the contemporary record reflecting 'the great relief expressed throughout Anglo-Ireland suggests that the battle may well have gone the other way'.[18]

Of no less significance here than the size and success of the Bruces' forces is the evidence – preserved in just two key annal references – for their having included some numbers of West Highland warriors. In their entries of Edward's death at Faughart, three annalists record that a 'MacRuari, king of the Hebrides (*rí Innsi Gall*), and MacDonald, king of Argyll (*rí Oirir Gaedeal*) and their Scots were killed there with him',[19] and thus confirm contingents from Argyll and the Isles having been among Edward's forces at the end. The entries in the *Annals of Connacht* and the *Annals of Ulster* of King Robert's arrival in Ireland two years earlier both notice his 'bringing many galloglas (*galloclaechaib*) with him' and can be taken as evidence for a substantial West Highland component in the reinforcements he brought to his brother's aid. The annalists' use of the term 'galloglas' in this instance seems unusual when elsewhere in the annal record it is consistently applied only to mercenary fighting-men from Gaelic Scotland resident in Ireland, and yet these warriors formed an expeditionary force from Scotland and were most unlikely to have been mercenaries.

It may be possible, however, to discern a strategic significance in the use of the term in that context and at that date if the meaning intended by the annalists was as simple as 'warriors from the Hebrides and West High-lands'. If that interpretation is correct, it is quite possible that the same meaning – bearing on their region of origin, and possibly also their appearance, but without any special emphasis on residence in Ireland – had been similarly intended by the few earlier annal references to 'galloglas'. In that case, the use of the term to identify a distinct mercenary warrior élite, established in Ireland but of Gaelic Scottish origin, would have been a rather later fourteenth-century application of the same word. Such a possibility would, in fact, correspond perfectly well with Professor Hayes-McCoy's conclusion that 'although there had been Hebrideans in Ireland before 1314, the coming and consolidation of the gallóglaigh in Ireland is bound up closely with the Bruce invasion'.[20]

Seen from that viewpoint, then, the Bruces' invasion of Ireland would represent a watershed in the emergence of the galloglas. It is almost impossible to imagine any Irish chieftain who learned of the invading Scots' victories against Anglo-Norman armies in Ireland or had himself taken the field as one of the Bruces' Irish allies having failed to appreciate how a force of that same quality and character might dramatically improve his own military capability. Nor would it have escaped his notice that there were such fighting-men already living in Ireland, and had been for at least half a century even if not yet in the numbers or the battle-readiness of those serving the Bruces.

The first arrival of those warriors can be attributed to the greatly increased contact of the Gaelic aristocracy of the West Highlands and Hebrides with the north of Ireland through the thirteenth century – including Scottish military interventions in Ulster – but particularly, it would seem, in association with marriage alliances between northern Irish chieftains and daughters of noble kindreds in Argyll. The earliest such record is the annal notice of the *oclaech* delivered with his MacRuari bride to Aodh O'Connor in 1259, and it might have been around that date that Donal Og O'Donnell – who had himself been fostered by the MacSweens of Knapdale – took a MacSween for his first wife. His second wife, a daughter of MacDonald of the Isles, evidently brought with her a company of galloglas who were, of course, the very first to be mentioned under that name by the annalist at 1290.

The implication of the first few notices of warriors recognisable as galloglas, then, is of their having served as personal guards to northern Irish nobility and, indeed, it was in that same capacity that the galloglas so vividly described by William Camden had come to London with Shane O'Neill in 1562. Inevitably, of course, such a guard would have accompanied a chieftain into battle and need not have attracted any notice by the annalists in so doing, especially when the use of mercenaries had been a characteristic of the militarisation of Irish society which had been in process since the death of Brian Boru at Clontarf in 1014.

As that process was accelerated and extended in the aftermath of the Bruce invasion, so the employment of galloglas – surely inspired in at least some measure by the performance of such warriors in the Scots forces – became its principal expression. The tides of the time in the West Highlands bearing dramatically on the fortunes of its principal kindreds assuredly played no small part in stimulating further migration of fighting-men to Ireland. It seems also very likely that warriors who had come to Ireland in the forces of the Bruce invasions – especially those whose chieftains had been slain – might have stayed on to reinforce the expanding presence of galloglas who are found ever more widely and in ever greater numbers as mail-clad heavy infantry on Irish battlefields through the fourteenth and fifteenth centuries.

'Better is a castle of bones than a castle of stones', advised Sir Robert Savage of the Ards in the fourteenth century. His 'castle of stones' makes clear reference, of course, to the policy of 'incastellation' by which Anglo-Norman lordship had extended itself across some three-quarters of Ireland, but by 'castle of bones' is meant the galloglas who came to represent the cutting edge – most often in the literal sense of that phrase – of the Gaelic resurgence. By the eve of the sixteenth-century English reconquest of Ireland, galloglas were found in the employ of native Irish and gaelicised Anglo-Irish lords in every province, not least among them the Fitzgerald earls of Kildare, who served as Henry VIII's governors in Ireland and yet appeared almost indistinguishable from a traditional Gaelic high-king. When more direct English government was imposed after the Kildare rebellion of the 1530s, the galloglas were again at the cutting edge of Gaelic and gaelicised Ireland's resistance and yet were also recruited into the Irish forces of the Tudor sovereigns. It being the essential tenet of the mercenary to fight for whosoever will pay him, galloglas were found not only on almost all of Ireland's battlefields until the end of the sixteenth century but fighting on both sides.

As they became ever more prominent as a military élite in its warfare, so the galloglas – subscribing to their own military ethos and singularly accomplished in the handling of their own characteristic weaponry – became recognised as a professional class in Irish society. Like other such classes in the Gaelic world – of which lawyers, doctors and bards are comparable examples – they were organised on the basis of kin-groups, each of which eventually attached itself to a lordly paymaster, the office of constable (as their commanders were styled) becoming hereditary in his service. This organisation and identification by kin-group is one of the most typically Gaelic aspects of the galloglas and so – before considering them as a specifically military phenomenon – it seems fitting to trace each kindred back to Scotland's western seaboard, seeking out the character of its ancestry and origins there as the background to its first appearance and subsequent progress in Ireland.

II

KINDREDS

'If the father hath beene a Galloglas, the sonne will be a Galloglas'

It seems to be in the nature of the historical record to reserve name-checks for the noble and notorious, and thus lose to posterity the names of such lesser mortals as hewers of wood, drawers of water and – more importantly here – rank-and-file mercenary warriors. One of the earliest annal notices of galloglas in battle occurs at the year 1316 where the entry of the defeat of a king of Connacht by a rival O'Connor lists the notables slain around the king and includes at its foot 'Duncan MacRory with a hundred galloglas'.[1]

Closely similar forms of entry of battles, concluding the list of important casualties with the name of the commander of galloglas (sometimes styled *consapal* or 'constable'), perhaps accompanied by that of his son or other close kinsman and followed by a note of the number of his warriors slain around him, become almost commonplace throughout the annal record of the following three centuries. With just one or two exceptions, the surnames of constables noticed in the annals are those of the six familiar galloglas kindreds, but the names of those in his company go unrecorded and so there is the least evidence of the identity or origin of the great majority of the ranks of galloglas. Certainly in the fourteenth century, it would be reasonable to assume some form of kin-group link with the commander, or at least of West Highland or Hebridean descent and background, for any such warrior, especially when the inevitable losses in battle could be replenished by further recruitment from the homeland.

By the later fifteenth century, though, when relentless demand must already have outstripped the diminishing supply from that source, it seems unlikely that Irishmen of suitable physique and aptitude would not have been recruited, probably in boyhood or adolescence, for training and service as galloglas. Indeed, there are entries in later sixteenth-century state records – predominantly those of Leinster and Munster – identifying men with unmistakably Irish names as galloglas. If the idea of a native Irish *galloglach* seems a contradiction in terms (as, in the strictest sense of the word, it must), then the ample evidence for galloglas having taken local wives from the time of their first settlement in Ireland should be borne in mind when it infers the wider extension of the kin-group by marriage as well as the mingling of bloodlines.

Nonetheless, the hereditary aspect remained a characteristic of the galloglas identity through all the generations, and the English soldier of fortune Barnaby Rich, who had first-hand experience of facing their axemen in battle during the Desmond rebellion of 1579, said of them that 'if the father hath beene a Galloglas, the sonne will be a Galloglas'.[2] Rich's observation is especially interesting in that it would seem to be applied to galloglas in general while the great weight of evidence from the annals and genealogies for their hereditary character bears almost exclusively upon principal officers as prominent members of their kindred. Nonetheless, when a constable of galloglas in the later sixteenth century could take pride in his direct descent from the first of his name who had arrived in Ireland at least two hundred and fifty years earlier, there is full justice in the recognition of these galloglas families as dynasties of a military aristocracy.

Of which, then, the first example must be the MacSweeneys who are widely acknowledged as Ireland's principal galloglas kindred and whose branches are found in mercenary warrior service across the full extent of the country from Donegal with the O'Donnells down to Cork and Kerry with the MacCarthys.

Clann Suibhne – The MacSweeneys

The earliest narrative account of the origin of the MacSweeneys is contained in the *Book of the MacSweeneys*, a history of the senior branch of the kindred – that of Fanad in Tyrconnell – completed in the first half of the sixteenth century.[3]

Its opening passages tell the story of a dispute between Donal and Anradhan, the sons of Aodh Athlomhan, king of Ailech, whose obituary is entered in the annals at 1033. Anradhan is said to have been the popularly preferred successor to his father, but his claim was overruled by his elder brother Donal who claimed the kingship by right of seniority (and, indeed, it was from this Donal that the later O'Neills were descended). Denied the kingship, Anradhan declined to stay in Ireland, setting forth 'with a troop in his company' and eventually coming to settle in Scotland:

And when they had spent some time in Scotland they enjoyed great prosperity and wealth, and wide conquest in all the country. They made peace and marriage alliance with the king of Scotland then in this way . . . the daughter of the king of Scotland was given in marriage to Anradhan and descended from these two are the whole of Clann Suibhne from that time to now.

The Sween (*Suibhne*) for whom the clan is named was the great-grandson of this Anradhan – and Sween's own grandson was the Murrough who became the first MacSweeney named in the Irish annals with the entry at 1267 of his death in the earl of Ulster's prison.

While there is reliable evidence to confirm the presence of MacSweens in Scotland – most prominently in the form of the twelfth-century Castle Sween in Knapdale – as there is to indicate the circumstances surrounding their relocation to Ireland in Murrough's time and after, modern Irish historians seem still to be unpersuaded by the MacSweeney claim to descent from the Cenel Eoghain kings of Ailech.[4] Their scepticism springs from a distrust of the evidence of the sixteenth-century clan history, which is not unreasonable when the earlier pages of that narrative include anecdotes of obviously unhistorical, and even transparently legendary, character. Such material, however, is hardly unexpected – even as late as the sixteenth century – in an Irish source drawing on old family traditions and evidently the work of a bardic poet, and so should not immediately discredit the genealogical content. There might be firmer ground for scepticism in the aggrandising tendency of the work, because its author was working to a commission from the wife of a MacSweeney Fanad chieftain and makes every effort to portray the family as a noble Irish dynasty. The term galloglas, for example, appears in just one passage of his work – in an apparently quoted text of terms for 'supply' of such warriors – and he tries wherever possible to present the MacSweeneys as 'allies' of greater lords rather than mercenary fighting-men in their employ.

There might be reasonable grounds for suspicion then, but not for dismissal of the claim to O'Neill descent when the same lineage is confirmed by genealogies preserved in the late fourteenth-century *Book of Ballymote* and the seventeenth-century collections of O'Clery and MacFirbis. All this evidence has been subjected to scholarly examination by the genealogical specialist David Sellar in his investigation of the origins of Knapdale and Cowal kindreds where he traces the descent of the Lamonts and MacLachlans – as well as that of the MacSweens – from Anradhan and argues convincingly for their claim to Cenel Eoghain descent being 'quite feasible'.[5] His paper leaves me, at least, fully content with the likelihood of an eleventh-century Irish origin for the MacSweens, although it might be thought to cast doubt over their emergence out of the Gaelic-Norse aristocracy of Argyll. In fact, there is no reason for it to do so because Sween the name-giver was the third generation in descent from Anradhan, all of them presumably resident in Argyll through at least a century and a half, so it would be reasonable to assume their intermarriage with older gall-gaedhil bloodlines.

Anradhan himself is said to have taken taken to wife a 'daughter of the king of Scotland', although which – or even what sort of 'king' – is not stated. It has been suggested that the lady may have been a daughter of Donald Ban, because Anradhan would certainly have been establishing his Scottish dominions during Donald's years of exile in the west (c.1040 – 1093), although it is no less possible that some unrecorded regional chieftain (who would have been recognised as a king in the Irish understanding of the term), and perhaps one of predominantly Norse ancestry, may have been the father-in-law. It should be said also that everything known of the marriages made by later generations of Anradhan's descendants in Scotland, and in Ireland too, does point to their association with the most prominent aristocracies.

The clearest indication of their intermarriage with gall-gaedhil stock occurs in the third and fourth generations in descent from Anradhan and it is based on the premise that the given name of offspring can usually be taken as an indicator of their mother's background. The *Book of the MacSweeneys* credits Anradhan's grandson Dunsleve with twelve sons (although very probably not by the same mother), four of whom can be identified as forebears of descendant kindreds in Scotland – and, of course, in the case of Sween,[6] eponym of the MacSweens and MacSweeneys, in Ireland also. Of the others, Ferchar was the ultimate ancestor of the Lamonts, Saibaran of the MacEwens of Otter, and Gilchrist of the MacLachlans. It is Gilchrist who is of key importance at this point, though, because the *Gille-* name-form has been recognised as 'indicating a Norse strain' in Gaelic families.[7] When two sons of this Gilchrist were called Gillespic and Gilpatrick, three examples of the same name-form are found within two generations, thus pointing to Dunsleve, and possibly his son Gilchrist also, having fathered offspring upon wives of gall-gaedhil descent.

Even disregarding such genetic and maternal input, there can still be no doubt as to three generations of descendants of Anradhan having been immersed in the same Gaelic-Norse culture and society which Somerled had come to represent by the middle of the twelfth century, nor of their having been prominent among its aristocracy before, after and during Somerled's ascendancy. While Sween's precise dates are nowhere recorded, he can be securely placed in the period around the year 1200 (the date assigned to the stronghold commemorating his name and thought to be the oldest surviving stone castle in Scotland), which would make him an approximate contemporary of Somerled's sons. There are very many indications of the Gaelic-Norse character of the *Clann Suibhne*, but the most impressive of all lies in their recognition as galloglas when the long-exiled descendants of O'Neill kings of Ailech finally came home in the profession of arms.

The first of the MacSweens known to have found his way back to Ireland – and the ultimate ancestor of all branches of the MacSweeney galloglas kindred – was the Murrough whose obituary is entered at 1267. The family had apparently maintained contact with the north of Ireland in the previous generation when Murrough was one of two sons born of his father Mulmurry's marriage to a daughter of Turlough Mor O'Connor, king of Connacht.[8] Mulmurry evidently succeeded to his father's lands in Knapdale, and the stronghold of Castle Sween with them,[9] but within his lifetime that lordship came under pressure from the feudal expansion of the earldom of Menteith which had passed to the Stewarts after 1258. A charter of 1262 indicates Mulmurry under Stewart overlordship, or even displaced from Knapdale, which would hardly have discouraged his son from coming to the support of Hakon's expedition of the following year, so there is good reason to recognise one of the West Highland chieftains leading the raid across the Arrochar portage – the man identified as 'Margrad' and associated with Kintyre by *Hakon's Saga* – as Murrough (*Murchadh*) MacSween.[10]

His appearance in the Irish annals just a few years later leads to the conclusion that the loss of his father's lordship in Knapdale and the failure of Hakon's expedition had prompted Murrough to seek refuge with his mother's people in Ireland. There he would seem to have become involved in a feud between O'Connor factions which led to his seizure by Donal O'Connor, his subsequent delivery to the earl of Ulster, and his death (quite possibly by deliberate starvation, a convenient means of execution of a noble prisoner in Ulster around that time) in the earl's custody in 1267.

It is perhaps surprising, then, that there is no swashbuckling account of

Murrough's adventures in Ireland to be found in the *Book of the MacSwee-neys*. Other than an identification of him as the son of Mulmurry and an anecdote concerning his direction of his father's funeral on Iona, there is no further detail of him and certainly no mention of his last days in Ireland. Instead the family historian moves on with speed to Murrough's nephew Eoin, 'the first MacSweeney who made a settlement in Fanad', and an elaborately unconvincing account of his adventures which is heavily dependent on elements recycled from elsewhere in Irish tradition, but still contains fragments of genuine historical value worth consideration here.

Whilst still in Scotland, Eoin is said to have been a foster-son of a 'MacGofradha of the Isles' and to have distinguished himself fighting in defence of their 'lands and patrimony', slaying sixteen foes in one encounter. Great emphasis is placed on Eoin's prowess as a warrior and, indeed, one of the cognomens given him is *Eoin an Engnamha*, 'Eoin of the Prowess', so the claims for his accomplishment at arms may well be based on a genuine reputation,[11] although no less probably exaggerated to emphasise the élite military character of the MacSweeneys from the time of their first arrival in Fanad.

It is interesting also to speculate on the likely historical identity of his foster-father 'MacGofradha of the Isles', because the name is a gaelicised patronymic form of Godred, a personal name most often found in the royal house of Man which was still in some kingship of the Isles until 1266. There was a Godred of that lineage who died c.1237 and another who was declared 'king' during an abortive rebellion on Man around 1275, so it is tempting to suggest 'MacGofradha' as a son of one of these who had fled Man to find refuge in the Isles. Whatever his true identity (or historicity), this MacGofradha is said to have come with Eoin to Donegal for the purpose of cutting ship-timber and whilst there to have been treacherously slain by the O'Breslins of Fanad. Eoin returned to Scotland, where he is said to have been appointed earlier by the king as 'his own champion' and to have fought in that capacity against the English (all of which is hardly credible, but does correspond to the similar role performed by prominent galloglas in Irish battles as late as the 1500s). Back at the Scottish court, however, Eoin is said to have slain a foster-son of the king and incurred the penalty of banishment from Scotland 'until the end of the year'.

So it was that he sailed from Scotland 'with a great fleet [and] the place where he landed was in Fanad' where he avenged the killing of MacGo-fradha upon the O'Breslins in 'the rout of Crann Cuillmin in Fanad, after which Eoin seized all the country and dwelt there ever after'. Therein, I suspect, lies the real purpose of this expansive account of Eoin. He was not the forebear of any subsequent branch of the galloglas kindred, so his significance in the narrative can only be as 'the first MacSweeney . . . in Fanad' with his adventures elaborated to contrive the kindred's claim to that territory by right of conquest. While it is true that the O'Breslin connection with Fanad disappears from the annals in the 1260s, the MacSweeney lands there were probably formally granted – as Katharine Simms suggests – by way of reward for the 'king-making role' played by their leaders in the O'Donnell succession struggle of the middle decades of the fourteenth century.[12]

The importance of Eoin in the real history of the MacSweeney galloglas might thus be considered rather less than that of his daughter Catriona, the wife of Donal Og O'Donnell who bore him his son and successor Aodh. The claim to that effect made by the *Book of the MacSweeneys* is confirmed by the annals which, of course, also record Aodh's having been deposed by his half-brother Turlough in 1290 'through the power of his mother's kin, the Clan Donald, and of many other galloglas'. If Donal Og's second wife had brought him galloglas, then it is reasonable to assume Catriona having earlier brought with her a similar dowry of MacSweeney fighting-men. Presumably they would have stood by her son Aodh after 1290 and returned with him when he was restored to power five years later, thus laying the foundation of the MacSweeney galloglas association with the O'Donnells which was to endure through the following three centuries.[13]

In fact, the most substantial evidence for the emergence of the MacSweeney galloglas is all found in the generation after Eoin. His sons are said to have followed him into the chieftaincy, the elder Turlough allowing his younger brother to succeed their father and claiming the succession himself when his brother died within the year. When Turlough was slain in battle with hostile neighbours,[14] his people crossed to Scotland with an appeal to their kinsman Murrough Mear for support against 'the men of Tyrconnell', but Murrough was distracted at that time by 'dispute and war' with the king of Scotland, upon whom he inflicted a great defeat in battle. 'Sruibhshliabh in Scotland is the name of the place where that battle was fought.' After this victory, however, Murrough gathered a great fleet and came with his son to Ireland where they fought a campaign of conquest in Fanad and other MacSweeney territories in Tyrconnell.

Although he appears nowhere in the annal record and the account of him in the *Book of the MacSweeneys* is in great part obviously fanciful, there is no reason to doubt the historicity of this Murrough. He is entered in the fourteenth-century MacSweeney genealogies preserved in the *Book of Ballymote* and the *Book of Lecan*, where he is distinguished from his grandfather, the Murrough of 1267, by the cognomen of *Murchadh Mear* ('Murrough the Crazy') and identified as the forebear of all the subsequent branches of the MacSweeney kindred in Ireland.[15] In its account of his earlier career in Scotland, the *Book of the MacSweeneys* supplies one key reference which points with unusual precision to the date and context of his arrival in Ireland and it is found in the name of the battlefield where Murrough is said to have fought against the Scottish king. *Sruibhshliabh* corresponds so well to the anglicised *Scrubleith*, by which name the *Annals of Clonmacnoise* call the town of Stirling in their entry of the battle of Bannockburn at 1314, that the two must surely be the same, and thus infer Murrough Mear having fought on the English side in that battle.

All of which (other than the claim for his having won a great victory there) is eminently plausible in the light of evidence from the Anglo-Scottish historical record for the MacSweens' loyalty to Edward II and opposition to the Bruce and his allies. It also tempts speculation as to the extent of Murrough's involvement in the turbulence surrounding the MacSweens in Scotland at that time, and especially in the 'tryst of a fleet against Castle Sween' commemorated in the memorable poem preserved in the sixteenth-century collection of Gaelic verse known as the *Book of the Dean of Lismore*. This poem celebrates an expedition led by an Eoin MacSween and is thought to describe a genuinely historical, although evidently unsuccessful, attempt by the MacSweens to reclaim the stronghold named for their ancestor and with it their patrimony of Knapdale. The editor of the published edition of the Lismore collection associates the events described in the poem with a document dated 22nd July 1310 by which the English king Edward II granted to '*Johannes filius Swieni de Ergadia* and his brothers *Terrealnanogh* and *Murquoucgh* the whole land of Knapdale which belonged to their ancestors, provided they could reclaim it out of his enemies hands', in order that they might make themselves 'more hateful to his enemy John of Menteith'.[16]

The *Johannes filius Swieni* – who, presumably, is the *Eoin Mac Suibhne* of the poem – has been identified as an Iain, grandson of Dugall (brother to Mulmurry) MacSween and there is no reason to doubt that identification.[17]

Perhaps rather less secure, however, is the acceptance of the two names entered by the scribe as those of Iain MacSween's brothers, because those same names clumsily rendered from the Gaelic in the document are also found – and at much the same historical period – in the *Book of the MacSweeneys*. There the clan historian identifies the elder son and eventual successor of Eoin MacSweeney as *Toirrdhealbhach* (Turlough) and his second cousin, at that time still in Scotland, as *Murchadh* (Murrough Mear). It is, of course, not unusual to find the same names recurring down the generations in Gaelic genealogies, and even in different branches of the same lineage, so the entry of two Turloughs and two Murroughs in two generations by two distinctly independent sources could be reasonably attributed to pure coincidence. On the other hand, a scribe as unfamiliar with Gaelic language and custom as the one who set down the names in the document of 1310 might have casually assumed three kinsmen with the same patronymic surname to have been 'brothers'. Had he identified Turlough and Murrough as 'cousins' to the Iain (or *Eoin* whose name he latinised as *Johannes*), then the document would have granted 'the whole land of Knapdale' to the chieftains of the three branches of the *Clann Suibhne* at that date – which may indeed have been its intention.

The inference of that possibility would suggest Murrough Mear having contributed his own galleys and fighting-men to that 'tryst of a fleet against Castle Sween', but however plausible it appears, there is nothing in the poet's text to indicate his having done so. There is, however, at least a fragment of evidence to suggest his having fought at Bannockburn – just possibly in some mercenary capacity, but assuredly on the losing side – so he would have faced only the bleakest of prospects in Scotland at the end of June 1314, and relocation to Ireland would have offered the brighter alternative for him and his people. Thus the claim made by the *Book of the MacSweeneys* for Murrough Mear's arrival in Lough Swilly at some time after Bannockburn begins to appear eminently credible. The precise date, of course, is beyond confirmation but can be placed within at least a few months or at most a few years of the summer of 1314, which fixes an especially significant period of Irish history to Father Walsh's proposal that 'from this time dates the permanent settlement by the MacSweeneys of Fanad'.[18]

The coming of Murrough Mear is most realistically recognised as a new and substantial influx of MacSweeney galloglas into Tyrconnell at the time of (or shortly after) the Bruce invasion, when the politics and society of northern Ireland were in some degree of turmoil and the demand for West Highland fighting-men was about to surge to unprecedented levels. There could hardly have been a more propitious time for their arrival.

It is still unlikely that Murrough Mear and his son achieved the widespread conquest claimed by the *Book of the MacSweeneys*, and Father Walsh doubted whether they could have 'occupied much territory in Tyrconnell other than the neighbourhood of Lough Swilly'. Thus the claim for Murrough Mear's bequest to his grandson of *Tír Baghuine* (Banagh on the south-west coast of Donegal) was probably invented as a device to link him more closely with the Banagh sept of the MacSweeneys which emerged in the early fifteenth century. The story of Murrough's departure on a voyage in quest of the 'Fortunate Isles' – another legendary motif familiar from elsewhere in Irish tradition – is quite clearly unhistorical, but his parting wish conveniently leads on to an account of his successor.

If he did not return within the year, says the narrative, his son was to inherit the chieftaincy – as indeed he did – and so the detail of the territory of that bequest 'leaving all his countries to his family, from the mountain [of *Bearnas Mór*] eastward, to his son Murrough Og' is of genuine historical significance. A passage in the *Annals of the Four Masters* at 1592 is one of the most specific references in the Irish sources to the Barnesmore Gap – north-east of Donegal town along the road to Letterkenny – as a division of the territory of Tyrconnell, which would point to the country between Barnesmore mountain and Lough Swilly as the extent of territory bequeathed to Murrough Og.

This, then, appears to have represented the core of MacSweeney territory at the time of his chieftaincy, a period of some twenty years (c.1320–40 in Father Walsh's estimate), but the claims made by the clan historian for 'conquest' and lordship do need to be treated with caution. While it would appear that galloglas kindreds had achieved some form of lordship of their own 'countries' – in some cases akin to that of a vassal chieftain – by the later period, their initial form of landholding in the earlier fourteenth century was more probably in terms of a scattering of individual townships as distinct from lordship of a wider extent of territory. Such modest land grants were probably made by lords needing to employ galloglas at times when their available resources would not extend to supporting expensive mercenary forces in any other way. There is a distinct indication of that situation in the *Book of the MacSweeneys* when it tells of Murrough Og's son and successor Mulmurry (*Maolmhuire*) who is said to have fought on both sides of the O'Donnell succession struggle of the 1340s, but most profitably as an ally of Niall Garbh:

> It was this Mulmurry who, with Aongus na Tuaighe ['of the Axe'] O'Donnell inflicted the defeat of *Achadh Móna* [Aghawoney] on Niall Garbh O'Donnell . . . And it was this Mulmurry who, having come to Niall Garbh out of the attack on the house of Finros [in 1342], obtained two ballys [townships] of *Magh Rois* [Moross].

There is another instance, though, when Mulmurry is said to have claimed two more such estates by way of 'an *eiric* for Turlough [son and successor of the Eoin who had been the first MacSweeney in Fanad] because no *eiric* had been obtained for him up to that time'. An *eiric* was the compensation payable to the family of a man unlawfully slain and its value was based on his social status, so the lands granted in respect of the death of Turlough (at the hands of hostile neighbours some thirty years earlier) bear testimony to his standing, and also to that of Mulmurry when he was able to claim that compensation so long in arrears. The *Book of the MacSweeneys* supplies evidence also for the wealth of the house of Fanad during Mulmurry's chieftaincy in its anecdotes telling of his generosity to the bards and describing the tribute of 'eight score of swords having hilts ornamented with gold and silver' laid on the altar of the local church every Sunday.

Another form of acquisition of land may very well have been in the form of dowry when galloglas chieftains married into native Irish families. Murrough Og, for example, took to wife a daughter of a MacGinley who bore him four sons of whom Mulmurry was one. His brother Donough (*Donnchadh Mór*) is also worthy of notice at this point because it was from him that the second branch of the MacSweeneys claimed descent.

This was the MacSweeney Tuath (*Mac Suibhne na dTuath*) who take their name from the district once known as *Tuatha Toraighe* located on the north coast of Donegal looking out towards Tory Island.[19] It had been the territory of the O'Boyles, but the last notice of an O'Boyle chieftain associated with the area is entered in the annals at 1360, by which time they had been in some wise displaced by Donough Mor's branch of the MacSweeneys. Donough's son Ewen (*Eoghan*) is mentioned in the annals at 1359 as one of those taken prisoner after the defeat of the O'Donnells by the O'Connors at Ballyshannon.[20] Ewen's son and successor Turlough Og was apparently still living when the *Book of Ballymote* genealogy was set down before 1400, but – other than the entry of his brother Donough who was drowned in 1413 – there is no further annal record of a MacSweeney Tuath until the sixteenth century. Meanwhile, the second half of the fourteenth century had seen a significant development in the history of the senior MacSweeney line of Fanad – and indeed of galloglas in general.

When Niall Garbh O'Donnell was deposed by Aongus Og in 1343, the *Annals of Connacht* claim Aongus to have had the support of 'the Clann Suibhne at large', which might be taken to suggest Mulmurry's changing sides once again in the contest for O'Donnell succession. Such, of course, was the professional custom of the freelance mercenary warrior, but it was to undergo some measure of reform in the following generation.

Mulmurry died in old age around the year 1356 and was succeeded by his second son Turlough Caoch who is notable as the first of the Fanad line to be mentioned by name in the annals, and indeed for much else besides. The *Book of the MacSweeneys* tells how his elder brother 'defeated the English and the Scots at Bun Putoige' but was himself killed in action 'without knowledge of his people in that battle'. Turlough also fought on that day and 'had an eye knocked out by the shot of an arrow' – hence his cognomen *Caoch*, 'the one-eyed'. Turlough's chieftaincy was in part contemporaneous with the lordship of Turlough O'Donnell – usually called *Toirrdhealbhach an Fhíona* ('Turlough of the Wine') – and their relationship, although ultimately fruitful, began on the worst of terms with Turlough Caoch and his brothers fighting on the side of the rival O'Donnell faction. Turlough Caoch himself is said by the *Book of the MacSweeneys* to have inflicted the defeat of Sliabh Malair on the O'Donnell and afterwards plundered the church lands of a Columban monastery 'in spite of him' with his cousin Ewen of MacSweeney Tuath. The clan historian is swift to mention Turlough's having made a generous endowment 'to Columcille' in reparation whilst his kinsman Ewen made no such gesture.

The *Annals of the Four Masters* at 1380 record the 'great victory' which marks the beginning of Turlough O'Donnell's ascendancy, and the same entry notices Turlough Caoch's two brothers taken prisoner after fighting in the forces of the defeated faction. A story in the *Book of the MacSweeneys* must be assigned to much the same period when it tells of Turlough Caoch setting out with the rival O'Donnells on an expedition to Derry and leaving his son to keep guard over their flocks of livestock. Turlough O'Donnell attacked the camp, carrying off great spoils and taking Turlough Caoch's son as his captive, but the young man bore himself in such proud defiance even while shackled that the O'Donnell released him to return home to his father.

This incident is presented as the turning-point in relations between the two Turloughs, when the MacSweeney Fanad, delighted by his son's safe return, set out in full force on a courtesy visit to the O'Donnell and was welcomed with a lavish display of generosity. The *Book of the MacSweeneys* lists the gifts bestowed by the O'Donnell in its customary anecdotal fashion as it does the enthusiastic adoption by Turlough Caoch of the O'Donnell's son as his foster-child, but the next passage reveals a distinct change in the character of its narrative, almost as if its author is incorporating passages from a written document. Such is very probably what he was doing when he set out the endowments of the MacSweeney with lands and privileges, including 'a gift in perpetuity from [the O'Donnell] himself and his posterity after him [of] the making of a circuit of Tyrconnell once in a year [with] the spending of three nights in each house in Tyrconnell'.

'And it was then' – continues the narrative in its first and only passage in which the term occurs – 'that a levy of galloglas was made upon Clann Sweeney.' The precise terms of that levy are set out in detail which will bear fuller consideration later, but its most important element at this point is the agreement by the MacSweeney to provide the O'Donnell with 'two galloglas for each quarter of land and two cows for each galloglach deficient':

> And previous to this arrangement no lord had a claim on them for a rising-out or hosting, but they might serve whomsoever they wished. It was the Scottish habit [of military service] they had observed until that time, namely each man according as he was employed.

The 'gift in perpetuity . . . of making a circuit of Tyrconnell' reflects a custom in Ireland – as elsewhere in Britain also, but in the much earlier medieval period – whereby a lord was entitled to a periodic round of visits to his subordinate chieftains, each one obliged to provide feasting and hospitality for him and his accompanying retinue. It was, in fact, a form of taxation and the 'circuit of Tyrconnell' privileged to the MacSweeney can be recognised as a grander form of the billeting of galloglas on the lord's vassals, a custom soon to be widespread throughout Ireland. In the event, it was while Turlough Caoch was engaged upon his circuit of Tyrconnell that 'a great sickness came upon him and he died'. The date – on the evidence of his obituary in the *Annals of the Four Masters* – was 1399.

Following the death of Turlough Caoch – 'a man of great knowledge, very violent and very generous' in the estimation of his obituary entered in the *Book of the MacSweeneys* – the succession passed to his son and namesake Turlough *Ruadh* ('the red-haired'), but not without opposition from his father's two brothers. While the clan historian supplies no more detail of their contention than a bald statement of its outcome – 'Turlough by violence assumed the chieftaincy in the end' – his next passage does carry the implication of the O'Donnell's involvement in the succession: 'He was the first MacSweeney whom the O'Donnell himself inaugurated'. The annal evidence suggests a political context in which the O'Donnell would have been anxious for Turlough Caoch's son to succeed his father as the MacSweeney, because he was then at war with the O'Neill and uncertain of the loyalty of Turlough Caoch's brothers at a time when he had most urgent need of his galloglas.

The succession of Turlough Ruadh, however, did first establish the custom whereby each new chieftain of the senior Fanad line of the MacSweeneys was proclaimed 'the MacSweeney Fanad' at Kilmacrenan, the traditional site of inauguration of the O'Donnells. Whilst in Scotland, MacSween chieftains are said to have been inaugurated by the abbot of Iona (styled *comarba Coluimchille* or 'successor of Columba'), but with no trace of Scottish evidence in its support that claim must be considered historically suspect. It is probably most realistically recognised as an invention, either an attempt to emulate the custom of the Clan Donald Lords of the Isles or simply a gesture of spiritual solidarity with the O'Donnells, who were of the same *Cenél Conaill* ancestry as Columba and so revered him as their patron saint.

Even so, the claim does bear testimony to the MacSweeneys' regard for their West Highland origins having endured into the sixteenth century when the history was set down, as also does another tradition, apparently still current when it was recorded in the *Book of the MacSweeneys*, which tells how the ship-timber cut on the first venture into Fanad had been disguised by MacGofradha just before his death with a magic mist to obscure it from view. Thus, while the timber's whereabouts remained unknown, it was remembered as 'the famous wood wherein the Clan Sweeney are fated to sail to Scotland at some future day'.

To both Turlough Ruadh and his brother Conor (called *Balbh* or 'the stammerer') is attributed great prowess as warriors, a claim which – in the case of Turlough at least – is supported by the annal record. He would assuredly have been present in Meath in 1423 when the Lord Deputy's English forces were heavily defeated by a coalition of the O'Donnell, the O'Neill 'and the Irish of Ulster in general', and the *Annals of the Four Masters* confirm the prominence of MacSweeney galloglas in the conflict. In 1434 he is given a valorous role in bringing what remained of the O'Donnell forces to safety after their defeat by the English in which Niall O'Donnell was taken captive. It must be said, though, that the *Book of the MacSweeneys* is hardly impartial as a military history, as is best illustrated by its claim for the battle fought against the O'Neill in the Rosses of Donegal in 1435 as a victory for the MacSweeneys. The detailed entry of that engagement in the *Annals of the Four Masters* records their crushing defeat by O'Neill's MacDonnell galloglas, although it does allow Turlough Ruadh full credit for his sturdy part in the battle. By then he was reaching the end of his life because his thirty-nine years of 'full lordship in his country' place his death around the year 1438.

Turlough Ruadh was succeeded as the MacSweeney Fanad by his sons – Rory, who died around 1452, followed by his brother Donal Mor whose chieftaincy was cut short less than four years later when he was slain by his nephews, two sons of Rory. The killing of Donal heralded a period of internecine conflict in the house of Fanad reflecting another O'Donnell succession struggle, this time surrounding Turlough Cairbreach who was proclaimed the O'Donnell in 1456. Turlough Cairbreach's ally Enri O'Neill had taken prisoner the rival O'Donnell claimant Aodh Ruadh and his MacSweeney constable Mulmurry, the last of Turlough Ruadh's sons, thus enabling Turlough Cairbreach to intrude Turlough, son of Conor Balbh, as the McSweeney Fanad.[21] Four years later, Aodh Ruadh and Mulmurry were set at liberty and gathered support to challenge the chieftaincy of Turlough Cairbreach. When their challenge came to battle, Aodh Ruadh won the day and was proclaimed the O'Donnell in 1461, his ally Mulmurry MacSweeney being inaugurated into the 'lordship of his own country' in the same year.

All successor chieftains of the MacSweeneys of Fanad through three generations were descended from this Mulmurry or from his brother Donal Mor, the last inaugurated MacSweeney Fanad being Mulmurry's great-grandson Donal who succeeded in 1570 and was still alive in 1619. The first of those successors, however, was the Rory who became the MacSweeney Fanad after his father Mulmurry was slain in battle in 1472. A full and generous account of Rory's achievements – his building of the castle at

Rathmullen as well as a catalogue of military triumphs – is set down in the *Book of the MacSweeneys*, which should come as no surprise, given that the book itself was originally commissioned some five years before Rory's death in 1518 by his wife Maire, a pious lady who also founded the Carmelite monastery at Rathmullen.

Through the half-century before Rory's succession, however, other branches of the kindred were emerging in mercenary warrior service elsewhere in Ireland as MacSweeney galloglas extended themselves ever further outwith the country of Tyrconnell.

Of the three principal septs of the kindred – often referred to as 'the three MacSweeneys' – the senior line of Fanad and the Tuath branch on the north coast of Donegal have already been introduced here. The third branch has also received passing mention by way of the doubtful claim in the *Book of the MacSweeneys* that Murrough Mear bequeathed lands in Banagh to his grandson Dugall when it is hardly possible that he would have held estates so far to the south-west by the first quarter of the fourteenth century.

While Murrough Mear's bequest of Banagh must be dismissed as an invention of the clan historian, it was a claim evidently based upon the evidence of the old genealogies because Dugall was the ultimate ancestor of the branch of the kindred which appeared in the early fifteenth century as the sept of Banagh. An entry in the *Annals of Connacht* at 1356 records this Dugall slain by an O'Connor and, although it offers no further detail of the circumstances, clearly indicates his having ventured as a freelance mercenary warrior into the O'Connor country of Connacht, which would well correspond to the cognomen of Dugall's son who was called Ewen *Connachtach*. It is also supported by the evidence of a genealogy in the late fourteenth-century *Book of Ballymote* which groups together six of Dugall's grandsons as the 'MacSweeneys of Connacht' (*Mac Suibhne Connachtach*). Father Walsh has identified the Turlough MacSweeney – whose obituary entered by the Connacht annalist at 1378 styles him 'high constable of Connacht' – as the eldest of these grandsons, and, more importantly at this point, has also shown that the family of *Tír Baghuine* 'were an offshoot of this branch' and descended from Turlough's nephew Mulmurry (*Maolmhuire*), son of Eoin na Lathaigh.[22]

Mulmurry's distinguished part in the great defeat of the English army in 1423, when he slew the knight commanding the Lord Deputy's army even though a hundred galloglas under his own command were slain, is noticed by the *Annals of the Four Masters* where he is identified as 'Mulmurry MacSweeney Connacht' and yet styled 'O'Donnell's constable'. The same annals enter his obituary at the following year where he is similarly styled 'Constable of Tyrconnell, weapon of the protection and bravery of the province', thus leaving no doubt as to his having relocated from Connacht and entered the service of the O'Donnell, where his descendants, settled in the south-west of Donegal, were known in the next generation as the MacSweeneys of Banagh. For which a key item of evidence is supplied by an entry in the *Annals of the Four Masters* at 1497 which styles Mulmurry's successor 'MacSweeney Connacht, that is MacSweeney Banagh, namely Ewen'.

The sequence of MacSweeney Banagh succession is more securely traced through the three generations from Ewen's son Niall Mor, and all but one of the sixteenth-century chieftains were sons or grandsons of Niall's sons, Aodh and Mulmurry Mor. As elsewhere in the history of the MacSweeney kindreds, there was internecine contention also in the Banagh sept, notably in the case of the last chieftain Donough Dubh who slew his second cousin Niall Meirgeach to become the MacSweeney Banagh in 1588.

So it was, then, that the 'three MacSweeneys' – the septs of Fanad, Tuath and Banagh – had become firmly established in the service of the O'Donnells and settled in their own districts of O'Donnell's country by the eve of the sixteenth century. Yet – as the emergence of the MacSweeney Banagh out of Connacht has already illustrated – one branch of the kindred had found its way beyond Tyrconnell to establish itself in Connacht by the middle decades of the fourteenth century. While Mulmurry, grandson of Ewen Connachtach, returned to Donegal and there founded the sept of Banagh, his brother Donal remained in Connacht, and it is from him and his sons that the MacSweeney septs of Connacht and Thomond are descended.[23]

This Donal – who is identified in the genealogies as *Domnall na Madhmann* ('Donal of the defeats', presumably a reference to those inflicted and not suffered) – is noticed by the *Annals of Loch Cé* at 1419 and associated with Rath Glas in Galway. From him and through his eldest son Murrough Mor are descended the MacSweeneys of north Connacht who had lands in the district of Tireragh in Sligo and served as galloglas to the O'Connors of Sligo and the Burkes of Mayo in the sixteenth century. From Donal's second son Ewen sprang the MacSweeney sept of Clanricard who were joined by an offshoot of the North Connacht kindred as galloglas to the Clanricard Burkes of Galway, and from his third son, Donough, came the sept of *Machair Connacht* ('the plain of Connacht', now Roscommon) who served as galloglas to the O'Connor Don.[24]

Donough's son, Conor, was the founder of one more MacSweeney sept which took service as galloglas to the O'Briens of Thomond (in County Clare) in the sixteenth century. Yet another offshoot of the MacSweeneys of Connacht – this one descended from Donal na Madhmann's brother, Dunsleve – made its way into what are now the counties of Tipperary and Kilkenny and into the service of the Butler earls of Ormond, the most loyal to the Crown and most English in character of all the Anglo-Irish nobility, and yet even they had to have their galloglas in the early sixteenth century.

Then there were the MacSweeneys who found their way south into Munster, but these were not of the Connacht line and are linked instead to the older kindreds in Tyrconnell. In fact, the earliest appearance of a MacSweeney in Munster is claimed for a grandson of Turlough Ruadh of Fanad, Brian by name, who is credited by the *Book of the MacSweeneys* with having 'inflicted the defeat of Cnoc na Lurgan on Cormac Dall Mac-Carthy'. No date is assigned to this Brian's emergence in Munster, but it can be safely placed in the second half of the fifteenth century, which would correspond to his son Mulmurry's having been with the MacCarthys (as the same source says he was) in 1520 when they defeated the Earl of Desmond at Mourne Abbey.

The seventeenth-century O'Clery genealogies, however, give three pedigrees for the MacSweeneys of Munster and all of them claim descent not from the line of Fanad but from the MacSweeney Tuath. Some of these were constables to the MacCarthy of Muskerry and settled around Macroom while others were in the service of the MacCarthy of Carbery further to the south of what is now County Cork, but MacSweeney galloglas were also found in the employ of the Fitzmaurices of Kerry and the Fitzgerald earls of Desmond. Indeed, when Gerald Fitzgerald, the rebel fourteenth earl, was reduced to a desperate fugitive abandoned by almost all his followers in the wilds of Kerry in 1583, his last remaining constable of galloglas refused to abandon him and was slain by his own men as they deserted to the English. The man's name was Goran MacSweeney.[25]

No galloglas kindred extended itself so far across Ireland as did the MacSweeneys, but there is one which has a strong claim to have run them close when it penetrated even into Leinster and – most remarkably – entered into English royal service there. Those galloglas, of course, were of the *Clann Domhnaill.*

Clann Domhnaill – The MacDonnells

'The parallel between the affairs of the MacSweeneys and those of the MacDonalds in Ireland' – in the view of Professor Hayes-McCoy – 'needs only to be mentioned to become strikingly apparent.'

> Impelled by a common urge, reckoning on a common livelihood as free-lance axemen, both spread from the north across Ireland, and one after another impetuous and active sons of warlike fathers set out to found new lines of professional fighters in new areas and under new overlords.[26]

If the parallel between the progress of the two kindreds is 'strikingly apparent' in Ireland, the same cannot be said of its extension back to Scotland nor of the circumstances which brought about their relocation across the North Channel.

While the evidence of the Scottish and the Irish sources supports a sequence of events in which the displacement of the MacSweens from Knapdale in Argyll was followed by their reappearance as the MacSweeney galloglas in Ireland, the changing circumstances of the Clan Donald in Scotland through the same period follow a quite different direction. Indeed, almost all that is known of the MacDonalds between Angus Mor's involvement with Hakon's expedition of 1263 and his son Angus Og's part in the Bruce's victory at Bannockburn in 1314 indicates the consistent improvement in their fortunes which was to lay the foundation of their Lordship of the Isles in the 1330s. There is one prominent MacDonald, however, who is reliably recorded in Ireland as the ancestor of the principal MacDonnell galloglas kindreds, but whose personal fate and fortunes in Scotland are surrounded by uncertainty, and he was Alexander (or *Alastair*), eldest son and successor of Angus Mor.

The account of this Alexander Og found in the seventeenth-century *History of the MacDonalds* – written in English and attributed to 'Hugh MacDonald of Sleat' – points to his marriage to 'a daughter of Macdugall of Lorn' as having ranged him with the MacDougalls against Robert the Bruce so that Alexander 'fought always against him with Macdugall':

The King besieged Alexander very strictly at Castle Sween till he was obliged to surrender the castle. When he was taken, he was confined prisoner in the castle of Dundonald where he died. They granted Castle Sween and all his lands to his brother, Angus [Og] of the Isles.[27]

The authors of the nineteenth-century history of *The Clan Donald* accepted this version of events, as have two more recent historians of the galloglas who found in it an explanation of the emergence of Alexander's descendants as constables of galloglas in fourteenth-century Ireland.[28] It must be said, though, that the Sleat historian's garbled account of Alexander Og is shot through with confusion, most obviously when it fails to distinguish him from his uncle, the son of Donald who is sometimes called 'Alexander Mor'. Nor was Castle Sween in Knapdale a MacDonald possession until the time of Angus Og's son, John of Islay, the first Lord of the Isles. The account is further confused in its identification of Alexander Og's wife as the daughter of John MacDougall of Lorn when she is known from more reliable sources to have been Juliana, daughter of Ewen of Lorn, and thus not John's daughter but his aunt. Still more importantly, that marriage appears to have been a source of contention rather than alliance between Alexander Og and the family of Lorn, by reason of their dispute over possession of the Isle of Lismore, which seems to have represented Juliana's undelivered dowry. Alexander appealed his claim on Lismore to Edward I in 1296 after his recent appointment as the English king's bailiff, a post he probably accepted in order to strengthen his hand against the MacDougalls who were then out of favour with King Edward. By the early 1300s, when the MacDougalls were reconciled with the king, Alexander Og had already disappeared from the historical record.

On the basis of all this and more, the Sleat historian's account is generally rejected by much current historical opinion which finds more convincing evidence for Alexander's fate in an entry in the Irish annals at the year 1299:

> Alexander MacDonald (*Alexandair mac Domhnaill*), the best man of his tribe in Ireland and Scotland for hospitality and prowess, was slain by Alexander MacDougall, together with a countless number of his people who were slaughtered.[29]

If this 'Alexander MacDonald' was Alexander Og,[30] his disappearance from the historical record would be immediately explained, and so too would the apparent succession of his brother Angus Og who styled himself 'Angus of Islay' (*de Yle*) – the form of title signifying the head of the Clan Donald – in a letter thought to be dated to the year 1301. Whenever Angus Og did succeed to the chieftaincy, it would appear that he also acquired his brother's lands and thus effectively disinherited the sons of Alexander Og. So much is suggested by the late medieval genealogies identifying those sons and including amongst them three names – Black John (*Eoin Dubh*), Sorley (*Somhairle*), and Turlough – which are to reappear in the Irish sources as founders of MacDonnell galloglas kindreds in Tyrone, in Connacht, and eventually also in Leinster.[31] It would seem, then, that some of the sons of Alexander Og MacDonald found themselves faced with reduced circumstances in Islay and Kintyre after the demise of their father and so chose instead to join others of their name who were already established in Ireland in the profession of arms.

The presence of MacDonnell galloglas in the north of Ireland in the last decade of the thirteenth century is confirmed beyond all doubt, of course, by the annal entry at 1290 recording Turlough O'Donnell's seizure of the chieftaincy from his brother 'through the power of his mother's kin, the Clan Donald, and of many other galloglas'. The annalists' association of MacDonnell galloglas with the O'Donnells (who were later so closely associated with the MacSweeneys) is explained by warriors of the Clan Donald having formed the entourage, or some part of the dowry, of the 'daughter of the MacDonald of the Isles' when she became Donal Og O'Donnell's second wife. That marriage offers its own illustration of the involvement of the MacDonalds of Islay with the north of Ireland which seems to have gathered momentum around Angus Mor and through the second half of the thirteenth century.

The O'Donnell's wife was almost certainly Angus Mor's daughter, and his second son Angus Og also chose an Irish spouse when he took to wife a daughter of the O'Cahan (*Ó Cathain*) of Derry.[32] So, too, the annalist's eulogy of Alexander Og as 'the best man of his tribe in Ireland and Scotland for hospitality and prowess' carries every indication of Angus Mor's eldest son's activity on both sides of the North Channel. Nor is there any shortage of evidence for Angus' own activity in the Irish orbit, and it is that which might point more precisely to the earliest entry of MacDonnell galloglas into Ireland – and also into the service of the O'Neill.

Angus Mor's Irish adventuring is described in a closely contemporary

Gaelic poem addressed to him and claiming that 'you have come around Ireland . . . rare is the strand whence you have not taken cattle'. The poet's claim finds impressive support in a letter of 1256 in which Henry III of England instructed his officials in Ireland to forbid entry into the country to 'Angus Mor or other Scottish malefactors'. A political dimension is added to what might otherwise appear as purely piratical activity by the interesting suggestion that Angus Mor may have 'entered into a mutual bond with Brian O'Neill',[33] whose rising in the 1250s has been suggested as a starting-point of Ireland's Gaelic resurgence. Taking that suggestion one stage further, it would not be unrealistic to imagine that such a bond might very well have included the assignment of West Highland fighting-men and thus brought MacDonnell galloglas into the service of the O'Neill before the year 1260.

All of this would correspond to the evidence of the *Annals of the Four Masters* which tells how Turlough O'Donnell was himself deposed just five years after he had usurped his half-brother's chieftaincy in 1290 and how he afterwards left Tyrconnell to find sanctuary among 'his kinsmen, the Clan Donald' with the O'Neill in Tyrone. There is clear evidence, then, for MacDonnell galloglas in the service of the O'Neill by 1295 and every likelihood of their having been so employed through the previous four decades, so it is hardly surprising that the first appearance of a son of Alexander Og in the Irish annals should indicate him as a fighting-man in the orbit of the O'Neill.

The entry in the *Annals of the Four Masters* at 1349 records 'Black John (*Eoin Dubh*) MacDonnell slain by Manus MacMahon'. The MacMahons of Oriel (now County Monaghan) first appear as a new military presence, even if of a somewhat bandit character, in the region early in the thirteenth century and afterwards achieved their own brief independence before becoming subject allies of the O'Neills in the later fourteenth century. While the annal entry makes no reference to this Black John as O'Neill's constable of galloglas, it is almost certain that he was, in view of the hereditary aspect of such an office and the same annalists' styling his son 'heir to the lordship of the Innse-Gall and High Constable (*Ardconsubal*) of the province of Ulster'. By this time also, it has been suggested that the MacDonnells may even have been already established in the townland of Dungannon in Tyrone where their stronghold was known to the Four Masters and to the MacVurich historian as *Cnoc-an-Chluithe* ('the hill of sport', now Knockinclohy).[34]

Black John's son Sorley – or *'Somhairle* of the sharp and pointed spears' as he was called in a bardic praise-poem – also met his death at the hands of a MacMahon. The entry in the *Annals of Ulster* at the year 1365 tells how Brian MacMahon, newly inaugurated lord of Oriel, appeared to seal alliance with Sorley by marriage when he persuaded him to 'put away O'Reilly's daughter and espouse his own . . .'

> Shortly after this, he invited him [Sorley] to his house to drink wine, and when he expected to get the wine, the treatment he received was this: Brian folded his arms about him, and seized him roughly and carried him out, and his hands and legs were crippled and bound together, and he was cast into a lough, and no further tidings of him were heard.[35]

The treacherous killing of his high constable aroused the anger of Donal O'Neill who joined with Sorley's uncle Turlough Mor MacDonnell 'and all his tribe in Ulster' for a punitive expedition into MacMahon's country, inflicting defeat on the men of Oriel, plundering their weaponry and cattle and banishing their chieftain into exile after taking his wife and daughter captive.

The MacDonnell succession after the death of this Sorley is uncertain. His son John is noticed by the *Annals of the Four Masters* in 1366 as the constable of galloglas defeated by the O'Connors, but makes no further appearance in the historical record and is thought to have been slain in that battle. It seems most probable that the office of high constable of Ulster passed to Turlough Mor, who was with the O'Neill in the attack on Brian MacMahon and is named by the annalists as commander of Donal O'Neill's galloglas in the war against the rival Niall O'Neill in 1366. The annals also record that Niall O'Neill's forces included a contingent of fighting-men brought in from the Hebrides under the command of Turlough's older brother Ranald, and the *Annals of the Four Masters* tell how those two sons of Alexander Og faced each other across a ford on the River Bann:

> Ranald, son of Alexander, the heir to Clan Alexander [presumably the MacAlisters of Kintyre[36]], arrived at this time from the Innse-Gall, to assist Niall O'Neill . . . both parties met close together, that is the troops of the Clan Donnell. And Ranald sent messengers to Turlough and his son Alexander, with their people, to request of them to permit

him to pass in honour of his seniority, and for the sake of their kinship, but this request was made light of by the others, for they advanced to the ford where they saw him crossing. Here they gave each other a fierce and stubborn battle, in which countless numbers were killed and wounded on both sides. One of Ranald's sons was killed by Turlough in the heat of the conflict; and Turlough's son Alexander was taken prisoner by Ranald's people, who considered putting him to death at once, but Ranald did not consent to this, for he said he would not be deprived of his son and his kinsman on the same day.

Whether or not the line of Black John died out with the death of his grandson John, son of Sorley, the chieftaincy of the Tyrone MacDonnells which had passed to Turlough Mor in 1366 was to continue in Turlough's line thereafter. Only two years later Turlough's son, Alexander Og, appears to have succeeded his father, who had either died or become too old for warfare by 1368 when the O'Neills again took up their feud with Brian MacMahon. The *Annals of the Four Masters* tell of another expedition led into Oriel by the O'Neill who was offered gifts by Brian as '*eiric* for the MacDonnell [i.e. the drowned Sorley]'. The O'Neill agreed to peace on these terms, but they were not enough to satisfy Alexander MacDonnell, who joined together with a rival MacMahon and without O'Neill's permission 'made an assault upon his [Brian's] fortress . . . and Alexander, son of Turlough MacDonnell, together with a great number of others, were slain on that occasion'.

The historical record of the MacDonnell galloglas of Tyrone appears sparse to the point of invisibility through the decades that followed the death of Alexander, son of Turlough. It seems probable that a son (and possibly also a namesake) of Alexander was the constable who is identified only as the 'MacDonnell Galloglach' with Ewen O'Neill in the annal entry of a savage battle fought through the night against the O'Donnell's MacSweeneys in the Rosses of Donegal in 1435. The line of descent reappears with greater clarity from the next generation, however, with the brothers Sorley and Gillespic – almost certainly sons of the 'MacDonnell Galloglach' of 1435 – from whom descend all the subsequent heads of the sept of Tyrone.[37]

The apparent break in hereditary succession to the office of constable to the O'Neill after the death of Alexander may be explained in some part by the appearance in Ireland of the founder of another Clan Donald kindred which was later to be relocated from Islay to Ulster. This was John Mor (or *Iain Mhor*, whose descendent kindred is called in the Gaelic *Clann Iain Mhoir*), a son of John of Islay, first Lord of the Isles, by his second wife Margaret Stewart, daughter of Robert II of Scotland.[38]

On the death of John of Islay in 1387, the Lordship of the Isles passed to Donald, the first-born son of the second marriage, while his younger brother John Mor inherited lands in Kintyre and on Islay, the latter estate including the fortress of Dunyveg. So dissatisfied was John Mor with this apportionment of the patrimony that he rose in unsuccessful revolt against Donald, who pursued him from Islay to Galloway and then banished him across the Irish Sea to Ulster. The substance of which John himself explains in a letter to Richard II of England written from Armagh and dated 25th February 1395:

> I would have your Majesty to know that MacDonald, Lord of the Isles, my kinsman . . . expelled me from my country even to your land of Ireland, whereupon I came to O'Neill's country and up to this have been sojourning with the said O'Neill in dire hardship as the world knows . . .

The letter concludes with a statement of his intention to come to Richard when he visits Ireland 'and offer myself as a liegeman is bound to do to his king . . . whether O'Neill come to your presence or not'. Niall Og O'Neill did indeed come to pay liege homage to the English king at Drogheda on 16th March in the same year, and the official record of the submissions confirms that – as promised in the letter – John MacDonald was with him.

Of more immediate importance here, though, is the style in which John Mor signed his letter of February 1395 as 'captain of his nation and constable of the Irish in Ulster',[39] from all of which which it would appear that he had been in Ireland for some time by that date and had entered the service of the O'Neill in the same office of constable left vacant by the death in battle of Alexander in 1368. There is a further significance in the annalist's earlier recognition of a 'high constable of the province of Ulster' as 'heir to the lordship of the Innse-Gall' if – as has been suggested – John Mor's title 'constable of the Irish in Ulster' represents a variant of that 'apparently normally held by the senior member of the Clan Donald resident in Ireland'.[40] The term 'constable' will bear later consideration in the context of galloglas command structure, but it should be said here that the word is of Old French origin and entered Middle English in the thirteenth century. Passing over to Ireland in the currency of Anglo-Norman military culture, it occurs in the Irish annals (in its gaelicised spellings of *consapul* and *consubal*) in the fourteenth century, initially in association with the MacQuillins who are now thought to have been brought out of south-west Scotland – probably from Galloway – and granted lands in Antrim by King John around the first decade of the thirteenth century.

Although they cannot be considered a galloglas kindred, the MacQuillins did serve the de Burgh earls of Ulster as commanders of mercenaries, and it was from their forces' being known as the 'Rout of the MacQuillins' that their territory in Antrim acquired its name of the Route. The office of 'High Constable of Ulster' can thus be said to have originated within the de Burgh earldom, the last MacQuillin being appointed to it by William, the Brown Earl, just two years before his assassination in 1333. Thereafter the earldom passed to the Crown, its mercenary custom of 'the bonaght of Ulster' lapsed into disuse, and the style of High Constable of Ulster was appropriated by the O'Neills for the commanders of their MacDonnell galloglas. The great attraction of that title for the O'Neills might well have been in its reflection of their cherished claim to descent from Niall of the Nine Hostages who is credited by Irish tradition with conquest of the province in the fifth century.

By 1351 the MacQuillins were accounted rebels, yet they still styled their head of kindred 'constable' through the 1360s and clung on to their territory of the Route until finally displaced in the sixteenth century by the descendants of John Mor of Dunyveg, whose fortunes had swiftly improved from the state of 'dire hardship' of which he complained in 1395. Within little more than five years of that letter to Richard II, John Mor had returned to Islay to become reconciled with his brother Donald, and had also acquired by marriage the lordship of the Glens of Antrim.

Like the MacQuillins and at much the same time, the Bissets (a name anglicised from *de Biset*) are thought to have come from south-west Scotland, probably from Carrick, to take up a land grant in Antrim. When John Bisset was slain in 1383 he left only a daughter, Margery, as heir to his lordship, and it was she who became the wife of John Mor – presumably while he was still in Ireland – to bring the Glens of Antrim into the possession of the house of Dunyveg on the eve of the fifteenth century. The colourful history of this branch of the Clan Donald on both sides of the North Channel lies outwith the scope of these pages because, despite John Mor's own sojourn as the O'Neill's constable and his descendants' emergence as a major force in sixteenth-century Ulster, they were not a galloglas kindred.[41] Initially by right of marriage, they were independent lords of their lands in Antrim, where – as was needful in that territory at that time – they themselves became employers of galloglas.

There is one last reference to John Mor MacDonald which has timely bearing at this point and relates to a curiously far-sighted passage from the letter of 1395 offering his services to Richard II as 'your captain and constable throughout all Ireland with as many armed men as you wish me to have . . . ever to be subjected to your orders and commands'. Within a hundred and seventy years of his writing those lines, a Colla MacDonnell of the Tynekille sept of the kindred – which had found its way into Leinster out of Connacht in the first quarter of the fifteenth century – was to be formally installed under the Crown as 'Constable of Her Majesty's Galloglas'.

At much the same time as Black John MacDonnell – and, presumably, his brother Turlough also – were establishing themselves with the O'Neill in Tyrone, another son of Alexander Og would have been making his own way in Connacht.

This was the Sorley whose name appears at the head of the list of Alexander's sons in the *Book of Ballymote*. While Sorley MacDonnell himself is nowhere noticed in the annals, four of his sons are firmly identified as constables of galloglas by the annal record of Connacht in the later fourteenth century. As was the case with his brother Black John in Tyrone, the evidence for Sorley's sons as constables in Connacht can be taken to indicate their father's having similarly followed the profession of arms in that province and, almost certainly also, in the service of the O'Connors.

The first of those sons to appear in the Irish historical record was the Donal whose death – and that of his own son with him – is noticed in various annal entries of the battle of Beltra Strand fought between feuding O'Connor factions in Sligo in 1367. Ten years later the annals enter the death in battle of Donal's brother, Sorley Og, and the entries at 1388 in the *Annals of Loch Cé* and the *Annals of the Four Masters* record the same fate suffered by a third son of Sorley MacDonnell:

Donal O'Connor made an incursion into the Plain of Connacht and burned Ardakillin [near Roscommon] and island Loch-Currigan [in Ardakillin Lough]. Donal Og MacDonnell, constable of galloglas, was slain on this occasion.

It would be incautious, however, to draw an exact parallel beween the situation of the MacDonnells of Connacht and their kinsmen who were so securely established as hereditary constables to the O'Neill in Ulster. There is no MacDonnell in Connacht styled 'high constable' in the fourteenth century, for instance, and so – while the Clan Donald historians seek to indicate brother following brother into hereditary office in accordance with the Gaelic custom of tanist succession – the true course of events may not have been quite so straightforward.

By the last quarter of the fourteenth century, the long struggle between rival branches of descent from Aedh O'Connor (d.1228) had reached the point of division of their diminished territory of Roscommon – itself subject to rival claims of overlordship from the MacWilliam and Clanricard Burkes – between the O'Connor Don and the O'Connor Roe. When the MacDonnells are found first in the service of O'Connor Roe and afterwards in the forces of neighbouring allies, it would seem most realistic to suggest their having followed what the MacSweeney historian called 'the Scottish habit' of mercenary warrior service, fighting within the orbit of the O'Connor Roe alliance but for whichever associated chieftain had need of their services.

When war broke out between the two O'Connors in 1397, the constable of galloglas to O'Connor Roe is indicated by the *Annals of the Four Masters* as Marcus MacDonnell, the last of four recorded sons of the original Sorley. The annals supply a complex account of alliances formed on both sides of the conflict – including the 'O'Donnell with the chiefs of Tyrconnell' who came to the aid of the O'Connor Roe in vanquishing the opposing forces. In the wake of that victory, a quarrel over plunder broke out between factions of the victorious allies and the O'Donnell tried to resolve the dispute, but cavalry from the defeated O'Connor Don alliance seized the chance to take advantage of a distracted enemy near Lissadill townland on the way to Sligo:

They afterwards came to a brisk engagement in which . . . Marcus MacDonnell and Dugall, his son and a great many others of their galloglas were slain.

Nor did the second recorded son of Marcus – Sorley *Buidhe* ('the yellow-haired') – long survive his father and brother. In the year after the ambush near Lissadill, the O'Connor Roe advanced with the MacDermots of Moylurg into the Clan Donough country of Tirerrill in Sligo. The entry in the *Annals of Connacht* at 1398 tells how the invaders took 'great preys . . . and their hired troops and young levies went off with their booty'.

> O'Connor, MacDermot, and Sorley Buidhe, son of Marcus Mac-Donnell, MacDermot's constable, deserted by their own men, were left with but a small following. The O'Connor Don and MacDonough, king of Tirerrill, each with his own following, came upon them in Cnoc-in-Chroma and routed them there. Sorley Buidhe and his people were killed there and O'Connor's right hand was severely wounded.

An entry in the *Annals of the Four Masters* at 1400 mentions a Donough MacDonnell as constable to another MacDermot of Moylurg. The annalists do not indicate the descent of this Donough, but he would seem to have been in some wise related – perhaps even a brother – to the Sorley Buidhe who had also been in the service of the MacDermots when he was slain two years earlier. Indeed, when Donough is noticed again – by the *Annals of Connacht* at 1413 – he and his galloglas are with the O'Kelly and O'Connor Roe at the siege of a castle in Roscommon, and it seems most likely that it was he who is meant by the annalist's reference to 'Mac-Dermot's constable . . . killed there by an arrow-shot'.

The association of this Donough with the O'Kellys lends its own support to his likely kinship to the sons of Marcus when set beside the same annalist's account of the battle of *Bel Atha Lige* (near Killegilleen in Galway) in 1419. It was there that the Clanricard Burkes heavily defeated a raid into their country by the O'Kelly whose forces included 'a battle of galloglas of the Clan Donnell under Turlough MacDonnell'.[42] Now this Turlough – who is securely identified as a son of Marcus – represents a figure of key importance in the history of the MacDonnell galloglas because it was he who was to go on to found the senior line of the MacDonnells of Leinster.

All of which evidence from the annals might be taken to indicate Donough's having followed his kinsman Sorley Buidhe as the MacDermot's constable and still being known by that title when he met his death in Roscommon in the service of the O'Kelly. Had Turlough, son of Marcus

MacDonnell, taken command of Donough's warriors after 1413, it would explain how he came to be in command of 'a battle of galloglas' in O'Kelly's forces in Galway six years later.

Turlough would seem to have been in Roscommon in 1417 – in which year his wife (an O'Rourke) was buried there on the evidence of her obituary in the *Annals of Connacht*. If he relocated to O'Kelly's country in south Galway when he entered O'Kelly's service, then he moved on again, probably about 1420 after surviving the great slaughter at Bel Atha Lige, because he and his son, John Carragh, are both established in the province of Leinster when next noticed by the annal record. There they had settled in lands between the mountains of Laois and Wicklow, assuredly attracted to the region by the ever more pressing demand for the services of mercenary warriors on the borders of the English Pale. It is indeed quite probable that the authorities of the Pale, finding themselves increasingly unable to defend their settlers against warlike Irish neighbours, would have acquiesced in, or even encouraged, the settlement of galloglas on their borders.

So it was that Turlough and his descendants became 'Constables of the Pale'. By the time of his death – entered in the *Annals of Ulster* at 1435 – he had acquired lands at Tynekille in Laois, and these were inherited by his son John Carragh whose obituary in the *Fragmentary Annals* of Duald MacFirbis describes him as 'the best captain of the English'. The annals and state records for the sixteenth century identify two other septs of the MacDonnells of Leinster, one established around Talbotstown in Wicklow and the other at Rahin in Offaly, both of them thought to be ultimately descended from Turlough and probably through offspring of John Carragh. When John Carragh MacDonnell was slain fighting in Offaly in 1466 he was succeeded at the head of the sept of Tynekille by his son Turlough Og, of whom the historical record of the last quarter of the fifteenth century supplies virtually no account until the notice of his death in battle against the Burkes of Mayo in 1503.

By that time, the MacDonnell galloglas of Leinster had long been finding regular employment in the forces of the eighth Earl of Kildare, the extraordinary Gerald Fitzgerald (called in the Irish *Gearóid Mór*) who governed Ireland on behalf of the English through some thirty years, formally as the Lord Deputy but in practice displaying an authority much like that of a traditional high-king. His dealings with the Irish magnates outwith the Pale were conducted in the manner of a Gaelic overlord, damping down dynastic rivalries, sealing alliances with marriages and – when it came to a passage of arms – steeling up his forces with galloglas.[43] The 'Great Earl' (as he is most often called) died of a gunshot wound in 1513 and it was in the following year that John MacDonnell of Tynekille, son and successor of Turlough Og, was also killed.

In the next generation, dramatic change was to overtake the government of Ireland. The Great Earl was succeeded by his son and namesake, in whose time relations with the English so deteriorated that he was to die as a prisoner in the Tower of London in 1534. The London government's attempts to restrain what it saw as over-mighty Irish subjects (of whom the Great Earl was the most obvious, but not the only, example) had led to the imprisonment of the ninth earl and to his son Thomas' rising up against Crown authority. This 'Kildare rebellion' was brought to an end within little more than a year when 'Silken' Thomas surrendered to Lord Grey in August 1535, but its detail is of less importance here than its consequences, because the subsequent imposition of direct rule from London was to bear significantly upon the MacDonnells of Leinster.

Professor Lydon has pointed out that it was the Great Earl of Kildare 'who, more than anyone else, was responsible for making galloglas a routine element in government service' when he showed the only way the Pale could be defended, given the limited resources available to Dublin, was by the use of galloglas as supplementary forces.[44] Their recruitment into government service was nonetheless an embarrassment when the presence of warriors of such unmistakable Gaelic aspect in the Pale represented a blatant contravention of the ban on Irish custom demanded since 1366 by the Statute of Kilkenny. A report on the state of Ireland in 1515 observed that the 'guard of the King's Deputy is none other but a multitude of galloglas', and two years later the Great Earl's son and successor in that office explained to the Earl of Shrewsbury that 'wherever the deputy goes it is usual for his galloglas to have their food in those parts, except at great hostings; otherwise he could not support them were the king's revenue six times as large'. This form of billeting of mercenary fighting-men on the populace – known as 'coyne and livery' – was the customary mode of supporting galloglas,[45] although never approved of by London or Dublin. Nonetheless, when Justice Luttrell expressed his disdain for the practice in 1537 even he had to admit to the general opinion that 'the borders [of the Pale] are best defended by kern and galloglas' – the latter, of course, being the MacDonnells of Leinster.

By the 1560s galloglas would seem to have become as necessary a component of English government forces in Ireland as for so long they had been in the hostings of the Gaelic and gaelicised Irish lords who represented the resistance to Tudor re-conquest. Thus some alternative to the distasteful 'coyne and livery' system – which had become truly oppressive in the hands of the Anglo-Irish lords – needed to be found for their support. Just such can be recognised in the royal grant of 998 acres in the townland of Tynekille with attendant privileges to Colla (or Calvagh in the Irish name-form), grandson of the John MacDonnell slain in 1514. For his part, Colla MacDonnell was to pay a substantial rent of twelve pounds and nine shillings and also to maintain twelve galloglas for service to the Crown. In the same year of 1562, Colla's eldest son received a patent of the land of Acregar, amounting to some 320 acres, for which he paid a rent of three pounds and eighteen shillings and was bound to keep four galloglas for the Queen's service.

Under those terms, then, Colla MacDonnell of Tynekille and his son became the first galloglas formally installed under the Crown and with the commission to attend with due notice upon the Governor of Ireland or his Deputy and 'to go upon any Irishmen bordering upon the foresaid country'.[46] It was whilst in action as 'Constable of Her Majesty's Galloglas' that Colla met his death in June 1570. In accordance with the government policy of appointing English-born administrators to key offices in Ireland, Sir Edward Fitton had become President of the Council of Connacht in the previous year, and his first military venture in that office was a punitive expedition against the Burkes of Mayo. When the government and rebel forces met in battle at Shrule on the Blackwater River, which marks the border of Galway with Mayo, galloglas were heavily involved in the action. So it was, by a coincidence ultimately inevitable in mercenary service, that two branches of the same kindred found themselves fighting on opposing sides when MacDonnells of Leinster assigned to the President's forces faced MacDonnells of Connacht who had re-emerged in the sixteenth century as galloglas to the MacWilliam Burkes.[47]

By the second half of the sixteenth century, when MacDonnell galloglas had been with the O'Neills in Tyrone for three hundred years, they were also formally installed in the Queen's service in Leinster, and back again on the battlefields of Connacht but now with the MacWilliam Burkes of Mayo.

The Sleat historian, however, claims that descendants of Alexander Og extended themselves not only into Connacht and Leinster, but also into Munster – where no evidence has been found of any galloglas kindred under the name MacDonnell. Taking account of the confusion so often found in that historian's account of events and the absence of any branch of descent from Alexander Og as galloglas in Munster, it may have been that he simply attached the wrong ancestor to another branch of the Clan Donald which did find its way into that province where it was identified by the MacVurich historian as 'the Clan Sheehy of Munster'.

Clann Sithigh – The MacSheehys

The first appearance of the name MacSheehy in the Irish annals is found at the year 1367 where a William MacSheehy (*Uilliam mac Sithigh*) is numbered – with Donal MacDonnell and his son – among a hundred and fifty galloglas slain in the battle fought beween rival O'Connor factions at Beltra Strand in Sligo.

William MacSheehy thus becomes the first of very many of his name who appear as galloglas in the annal record of Connacht and, later, that of Munster through to the end of the sixteenth century. Their recognition by the annalists as galloglas supplies its own proof of their West Highland or Hebridean origin, and yet there is no record of a kindred in Scotland known by any form of the name MacSheehy from whom their descent might be traced. There is, however, a reference in the MacVurich history which points to their Clan Donald descent, and it occurs in the list of the sons of the eponymous Donald himself:

> He had good children, that is Angus Mor, the heir, and Alexander (*Alasdair*), from whom descended . . . the Clan Sheehy (*Clann Sithigh*) of Munster, who are sprung from *Siothach an Dornan*, son of Hector (*Eachuin*), son of Alexander.

The line of descent of the MacSheehys would thus be immediately explained were it not for the absence of collaborative evidence for this *Siothach* (a personal name extremely rare, if not entirely unknown, in old Gaelic pedigrees) from any earlier genealogy.

There is reliable evidence for Alexander's son Hector (as *Eachann* or *Eachand*) across a range of fifteenth-century genealogical sources, as there is also for his two sons who are named as Turlough and Lachlan, but no notice of the name 'Siothach' (or Sithigh). The nineteenth-century Clan Donald historians sought to solve this disparity by assuming that the MacVurichs had evidence of a third son unknown to any other authority, but David Sellar's more recent study of the genealogies makes the persuasive suggestion that *Siothach an Dornan* 'may be a by-name for one of the sons named in the genealogies'.[48]

All that can be said with security, then, of the eponym of the Clan Sheehy is that he was one of the sons of Hector MacDonald. As to the date and circumstances of his presumed relocation to Ireland, they are open to speculation for which the starting point must be the fragment of annal evidence for the William MacSheehy slain in 1367.

The genealogies place Hector in the same generation as Alexander Og, thus making his sons approximately contemporary with Alexander's sons who founded the MacDonnell galloglas kindreds, and would infer Sithigh having come to Ireland at much the same time as they. It may have been that he was the second son with only modest prospects in Scotland but of sufficiently warlike inclination to make his own way as a mercenary fighting-man in Ireland, but it is perhaps more likely – as Professor Hayes-McCoy has suggested – that he 'came over for some reason connected with the Bruce expedition'.[49] That likelihood is in some measure supported by the annal record of the death of Edward Bruce at Faughart in 1318, and in particular the entries in the *Annals of Ulster* and the *Annals of Connacht* which identify a 'MacDonald, king of Argyll . . . killed there with him'. The corresponding entry in the *Annals of Innisfallen* helpfully supplies the given name of the MacDonald as Alexander and has led to the suggestion of his having been the son – and heir – of Angus Og.[50] While that identification is less than conclusive, the evidence for a Clan Donald contingent in Edward Bruce's forces of 1318 remains beyond doubt and opens up the possibilities of its having included a son of Hector, of that son's having survived the slaughter at Faughart and thereafter chosen to settle in Ireland as a mercenary warrior. It seems likely also that it was in Ireland that he acquired the by-name 'Sithigh'.

He – and, assuredly also, others with him – would have been attracted to Connacht where an apparent surge in demand for galloglas was under way through the first half of the fourteenth century.[51] Had he taken an Irish wife who bore him a son in the years after 1318, it would be fully plausible to recognise that son in the *Uilliam mac Sithigh* noticed by the annalist among the galloglas slain at Beltra Strand in 1367. Even in modern Gaelic Scotland, a son is quite often assigned his father's nickname as a colloquial patronymic, and there is every likelihood of the surname 'MacSheehy' having come into use in just that way. Rather more unusual, in fact, is the given name of William (gaelicised as *Uilliam* by the annalist) which is of such distinctly Anglo-Norman character that it might be taken to suggest his mother having been of an Anglo-Norman family, especially when it is quite unknown in the earlier Clan Donald pedigrees, nor does it occur again in the annal record of subsequent MacSheehys.

Another thirty years pass before any further reference to the name MacSheehy appears in the annals, but when it does it is found again in Connacht and in immediate association with the MacDonnell galloglas in the service of O'Connor Roe, when the Four Masters (and the *Annals of Clonmacnoise*) notice a John (*Eoin*) MacSheehy slain alongside Marcus O'Donnell and his son in the ambush near Lissadill. Such inference as can be drawn from those two annal entries suggests the earliest generations of the MacSheehys established in Connacht as MacDonnell galloglas. Indeed, they were probably only noticed by name in the annals by reason of their eponym's own celebrity and high-born Clan Donald descent.

In fact, the emergence of the MacSheehys as a galloglas kindred in its own right is most safely assigned to the first quarter of the fifteenth century. The entry of the formal obituary of a Murrough Og MacSheehy in the *Annals of Connacht* at 1404 can be taken as evidence for this Murrough's having been a person of prominence and, in all probability, a constable of galloglas. Such an interpretation would well correspond to the appearance of the first reference to the 'Clan Sheehy' – which must indicate full recognition of the MacSheehys as a galloglas kindred – in the same annalist's entry at 1407 of 'a victory by O'Connor Roe and O'Kelly in which some of the Clan Sheehy (*Clann Sithigh*) were killed'. It would have been helpful to know if their commander was a close kinsman, or even a son, of the recently deceased Murrough Og, so it is unfortunate that the annalist's brief entry concludes with his statement that 'I do not know their names'.

An indubitable watershed in the progress of the MacSheehys can be placed around the year 1420 on the evidence of a reference in a manuscript pedigree of the Fitzgerald earls of Desmond which records the seizure of the earldom from his nephew by James Fitzgerald. This James – called 'the

Usurper' and destined to become the forebear of the subsequent earls – took to wife one Mary, a daughter of the MacWilliam Burke of Clanricard, and the manuscript goes on to explain that 'with this Mary came the galloglas of the MacSheehys first into Munster out of Connacht'.[52]

By the first quarter of the fifteenth century, then, the Clan Sheehy had begun to move southward, first of all into Galway where it entered the service of the Clanricard Burkes. So too it was – seemingly in the almost traditional form of an armed escort to a new bride – that the first contingent of the MacSheehys were brought across the Shannon into Munster. John O'Donovan, editor of the *Annals of the Four Masters*, is confident that 'the first of this family who came to Munster settled in the county of Limerick as leader of the galloglas to the Earl of Desmond in 1420'.[53] He claims also – apparently drawing on further evidence preserved in the Geraldine papers – that it was this same constable who built the castle of 'Lisnacullia' (or 'Woodfort') at Cloonagh in Limerick. He may well be correct, because the MacSheehys had certainly been drawn into Munster and into the service of the earls of Desmond in substantial numbers by 1535, at which year an entry in the *Annals of the Four Masters* mentions 'a large battle of the Clan Sheehy' slain in Limerick.

Nonetheless, some MacSheehys appear still to have been retained in the service of the Clanricard Burkes in 1522 when they suffered heavy losses at the battle of Knockavoe. The war of that year was fought between the O'Donnell and the O'Neill – the latter supported by an alliance which included the earl of Clanricard – and the slaughter at Knockavoe is presented by the annals as its most dramatic passage of arms. It was certainly one of the most ferocious of all galloglas engagements, being fought through the night when MacSweeneys (in the service of the O'Donnell) attacked the O'Neill camp at the head of Lough Foyle defended by MacDonnells and MacSheehys. The account of the conflict in the *Annals of the Four Masters* tells how 'O'Neill and his army were defeated and the camp was left to O'Donnell . . .':

> Great indeed was the slaughter made upon O'Neill in that place, for it was calculated by the people of the churches in which many of them were interred . . . that upwards of nine hundred of O'Neill's army fell in that engagement, so that the name and renown of that victory spread over all Ireland. The most distinguished men who fell in that engagement [included] Turlough MacSheehy with a great

number of his people . . . There came not a leader of a band or troop
in that muster of O'Neill who did not complain of the number of his
people left [dead] on that field.

Bitter memories of Knockavoe were passed down the succeeding generations and between different branches of the galloglas kindreds involved
which served to fuel a virtual blood-feud (a phenomenon far from
uncommon among galloglas kindreds) between the MacSheehys and
MacSweeneys.

By the second half of the sixteenth century – and especially through the two
Desmond rebellions of 1569–73 and 1579–83 – the MacSheehys were
predominantly associated with the Fitzgerald earls of Desmond. Indeed,
it was the unshakeable attachment of Gerald, the fourteenth earl, to his
galloglas which became one of his great points of contention with the
Crown authorities whose determined policy was demilitarisation of the
Irish lordships. Yet it must be said that the stories of the MacSheehys'
personal loyalty to their 'Rebel Earl' attribute an unexpected aura of
nobility to their mercenary profession of arms.

When Gerald was taken captive by the rival Butlers of Ormond after the
battle of Affane in 1565, he was carried off to London where he spent the
next seven years as a prisoner of the Queen. Eventually returned to Ireland,
he had little difficulty in escaping from Dublin and making his way south
into Munster where his principal constable, Maurice MacSheehy, was the
very first to greet him. Through the following decade, Gerald became the
inevitable focus of the second Desmond rebellion and, no less inevitably,
MacSheehy galloglas formed the cutting edge of his forces and his own
personal bodyguard. When he was pressed hard by the English commander
Sir John Zouche in April 1582 and defended by just eighty galloglas, his
camp near Kilfinnane was attacked by enemy troops. After a brief fight
which left half his small force dead, the Earl narrowly escaped capture when
four of his galloglas managed to carry him in a blanket across a peat bog to
safety. 'The dampness of the spring had paralysed his hip', explains the
New York historian Richard Berleth in his account of the Desmond
rebellion, 'so he was hardly able to walk or sit a horse, and again the
MacSheehy galloglas paid for his freedom with their lives.'[54] There is an
irony, then, in the story from the last days of the Earl which tells of his
being abandoned by all except the one last constable slain by his own troops

when he refused to join their desertion, because that man is said to have been not a MacSheehy but one of the disaffected MacSweeneys drawn to join the Desmond rebellion.

Eventually, though, the Clan Sheehy paid heavily for their loyalty to the Fitzgeralds of Desmond. When the second rebellion had been crushed, the Earl slain and his territory wasted by warfare, survivors of his MacSheehy galloglas made their way back to the lands in Glen Awbeg which had been home to their ancestors through three generations, only to find surveyors already at work in preparation for a new Munster plantation of English settlers. There was little left to most of them other than the outlawry of the dispossessed, and so the last appearances of the name MacSheehy in the annals of the sixteenth century are almost all of them found in entries bearing on one form or another of offence and retribution.

The claim made in the Geraldine manuscript for the Clanricard bride of an earl of Desmond having brought with her the first MacSheehy galloglas 'into Munster out of Connacht' represents a late – if not, indeed, the last – echo of the very earliest record of Hebridean fighting-men brought to Ireland with the daughter of Dugall MacRuari when she arrived to marry Aodh O'Connor in 1259.[55] That same annal entry must also be considered, then, as the first evidence of the presence in Ireland of what was to be known in the fourteenth century as the MacRory galloglas.

Clann Ruaidhri – The MacRorys

The eponym of the MacRuaris in Scotland (and the MacRory galloglas in Ireland) was the brother of the Donald for whom the Clan Donald is named: Ruari, son of Ranald and grandson of Somerled. The historical record of this Ruari begins with the entry in the *Annals of Ulster* of a battle in 1209 in which 'the sons of Ranald, son of Somerled, [i.e. Ruari and Donald] made a great slaughter of the men of Skye'. In the following year the *Chronicle of Man* records 'Angus, son of Somerled, slain with his three sons', both entries apparently referring to the 'warfare in the Hebrides' mentioned (although with no further detail) in the *Icelandic Annals* at 1210. Those three references taken together have been recognised as the record of a conflict between branches of descent from Somerled in which Ranald's sons, Donald and Ruari, slew their uncle Angus and his sons. Had Ruari gained territory in the north of Argyll as his fruit of victory, that would explain the association of his descendants with Garmoran and its outlying islands of Rum, Eigg, Barra and the Uists. Charter evidence from the early thirteenth century confirms Ruari's having already held lands in Kintyre, presumably inherited from his father, which would have provided the base for his raiding of Derry, Coleraine and Inishowen noticed by entries in the *Annals of Ulster* at 1212 and 1214.

In Scotland, however, the year 1214 saw the death of William the Lion, the succession of his son as Alexander II, and the customary challenge from rival Moray-connected factions sparking a sequence of uprisings which was only finally extinguished in 1230. The association of Somerled and his house with Gaeldom's hostility to the descendent successors of Malcolm Canmore goes back to the 1150s, so it is hardly surprising to find a 'Roderic' (the Latin form of the Gaelic *Ruari*) accused by the *Chronicle of Lanercost* of taking a prominent part in the rising of 1230. There would be good reason, then, to suspect his involvement in the earlier rising of 1215, which would well explain why Alexander II's intervention in Argyll of 1221–2 appears to have displaced Ruari from his lands in Kintyre and why Ruari's sons emerged as lords of Garmoran in the second half of the thirteenth century.

Ruari's son and successor Dugall would seem also to have inherited from his father the rebel streak he displayed in his determined allegiance to Norway both before and after Hakon's expedition to Largs in 1263. He certainly followed his father's example in his activities around the Irish coast – on the evidence of the reference in the *Annals of Loch Cé* to his having brought a 'great fleet from the Innse-Gall' to the coast of Connemara in 1258. Dugall first plundered a merchant ship of its cargo, and afterwards defeated and slew the Anglo-Norman sheriff of Connacht who came with his forces in pursuit of the raiders.

For all the annalist's description of Dugall's departure 'to his own country with joy and profit from triumphant victory', what might first appear as a purely piratical venture cannot have been without its political dimension when Dugall's daughter arrived in Ireland to become the wife of Aodh O'Connor of Connacht in the very next year. 'Once again', observes R. Andrew McDonald in his history of the kingdom of the Isles, 'it is the marriage alliances made by these Hebridean chieftains which best illuminate their allegiances',[56] and thus associate Dugall MacRuari, like his cousin Angus Mor MacDonald, with the Gaelic lords of the north of Ireland in the earliest period of their resurgence.

Those marriage alliances also introduced into Ireland the first contingents of Hebridean and West Highland fighting-men who were to become the galloglas. 'Eight score warriors' are said by the annalist to have accompanied Dugall's daughter to Derry in 1259, and the *Annals of Loch Cé* later refer to her husband as *Aodh na-nGall*, 'almost certainly' – in the opinion of Professor Lydon – 'associating him with the import of the "foreign soldiers" from the Innse-Gall'.[57]

So it must have been that the hundred and sixty warriors brought to the O'Connor with his new bride formed the nucleus of the MacRory galloglas found in Connacht through the fourteenth century. The annalist implies Alan MacRuari, uncle of the bride, to have been in command of this first company of warriors, but at some point afterwards he returned to Scotland where he became lord of Garmoran on Dugall's death in 1268 – and, indeed, it was to Alan's descendants that the lordship passed thereafter. One of Dugall's own sons – known as Erik in the Norwegian sources – sailed north with Hakon's fleet on its return from the expedition of 1263 and settled in Norway.

Dugall's other son, identified by the MS 1467 as Duncan, may well have been one of the young warriors brought to Connacht in 1259 and afterwards assumed their command as the O'Connor's constable. The same genealogy records his having a son also called Duncan who was, in all probability, the 'Duncan MacRory with a hundred galloglas' numbered by the Connacht annalist among those slain beside Aodh O'Connor's successor in battle with a rival O'Connor faction in 1316. In the following year, a constable identified only as 'MacRory the Galloglach' by the *Annals of Ulster* was slain with a hundred and fifty of his warriors when 'the men of Breifne' were defeated at Kilmore in County Cavan.

By which time, of course, the Bruce invasion of Ireland had been under way for three years and was soon to meet with its final defeat at Faughart in 1318. The annal entries which notice the death of Alexander MacDonald in Edward Bruce's last battle also name a 'MacRuari, lord of the Innse-Gall' slain there with him, and this 'MacRuari' is thought to have been Ruari, son of Alan. Alan himself had disappeared from the historical record more than twenty years before that date, so what is known of his two sons and a daughter charts the course of the MacRuaris through the 1290s and into the Bruce ascendancy. One of those sons was the Lachlan, described by the Clan Donald historians as a 'buccaneering predator',[58] who was ravaging Skye and Lewis with his brother Ruari in 1297 and afterwards on a northern rampage with the Comyns. The Earl of Ross complained of Lachlan's rebellious arrogance in a letter written to Edward II in 1308, but no more is known of him thereafter. His brother Ruari, meanwhile, apparently submitted to the English king before following his sister Christiana, the 'Lady of the Isles', in her enthusiastic support of the Bruces, which course eventually brought Ruari to his death in battle at Faughart, and left his troops – like those of the MacDonald slain beside him – at large in an Ireland ever more eager to recruit such warriors as galloglas. There is every likelihood, then, of the MacRory galloglas in Connacht having attracted substantial reinforcements in the aftermath of 1318.

When Ruari's son Ranald was murdered by the Earl of Ross in 1346, his lordship passed to his sister Amy and thence to her husband John MacDonald of Islay, the first Lord of the Isles. 'It is not all unlikely', suggests Professor Hayes-McCoy, 'that some sections of the Clan Rory were displaced by the failure of male heirs in the leading branch, and that they sought a livelihood in Ireland.'[59] However plausible that suggestion, I have been unable to find annal evidence for the continuing presence of MacRory galloglas, at least under that name, into the second half of the fourteenth century. In fact, the last notice of a MacRory constable in the *Annals of Connacht* is found in the entry at 1342 which records the O'Connor of Connacht defeated in Roscommon by an alliance gathered around the MacDermot of Moylurg who 'killed some of O'Connor's galloglas with their constable MacRory'.

The apparent disappearance of the MacRory galloglas kindred is most realistically interpreted as the last in a line of hereditary constables having been slain and leaving no capable male successor. As to his surviving warriors, the likelihood must be of their having been recruited into the forces of other constables, and probably – by reason of extended kinship – those of the MacDonnells of Connacht.

'Of galloglas commanders on record, those of the race of Sumarlidi far outnumber all the rest together' – in the estimation of Eoin MacNeill writing more than eighty years ago.[60] He may well be corrrect because, even without checking the precision of his calculation, it is clear that the names of no fewer than four of the six galloglas kindreds are those of branches of descent from Somerled of Argyll. The eponyms of the MacDonnells and MacRorys were grandsons of Somerled, and the Mac-Sheehys' descent from a great-grandson of the first of those grandsons is attested by the most respected source of Clan Donald tradition. It is the fourth of those galloglas kindreds, however, which was the last to be noticed in the annal record and yet has the first claim to seniority in 'the race of Sumarlidi', because the Dugall for whom the *Clann Dubhgaill* is named was his eldest son who inherited his lordship of Argyll.

Clann Dubhgaill – The MacDowells

An entry found in three Connacht annals at the year 1247 tells of a battle fought at a ford on the river Erne near Ballyshannon on the southern border of Donegal between an invasion force led by the Anglo-Norman magnate Maurice Fitzgerald and a defensive alliance mustered against him by the O'Donnells. When a cavalry manoeuvre won the day for the invaders, the annalists number among the slain 'all the chief men of the Cenel Conaill' – and with them a 'MacSomurli, king of Argyll'.[61]

While the annal reference is less than helpful in the identification of this 'MacSomurli', there is good reason to believe his having been Duncan of Lorn, son and successor of Dugall, son of Somerled. Other evidence places the date of Duncan's death at some point between 1237 and 1248, and the annalist's styling of the slain 'MacSomurli' as 'king of Argyll' points quite firmly to the territory of the MacDougall lordship in the mid-thirteenth century. If it was Duncan MacDougall who met his death fighting for the O'Donnells in 1247, his alliance with one of the Gaelic lords of the north of Ireland would align with the similar policy followed by his MacDonald and MacRuari kinsmen in that period.

Unlike them, however, there is no record of any marriage arranged to seal the house of Argyll into an Irish alliance, and so no convenient evidence of West Highland warriors brought to Ireland by a MacDougall bride. When the earliest notice of any MacDowell galloglas is not found until a full hundred and thirty years after the presumed date of Duncan's death at Ballyshannon, their emergence in Ireland must be placed in a later historical context, and there it can be recognised as a consequence of the determined opposition of the MacDougalls in Scotland to the rise of Robert the Bruce to kingship. The root of that hostility lay in the marriage of Duncan's grandson Alexander to a daughter of John Comyn, himself kin by marriage to the Balliols, which naturally drew the MacDougalls into the anti-Bruce camp. Its quite specific trigger, however, is generally recognised in the murder of John Comyn by Robert the Bruce in 1306.

The Bruce's career between 1306 and 1309 has been widely investigated in greater detail than is necessary here, but some account of his conflict with the house of Argyll will be helpful because it supplies virtually all that is known of the background to the MacDowell galloglas. In summary, then, King Robert I was crowned at Scone on 25th March 1306 and little more than a month after his murder of the Red Comyn, but within three more months he had become a fugitive. Defeated by the English at Methven near Perth in June, the Bruce and his surviving forces tried to break out to the west but found their route blocked at the head of Strathfillan by the MacDougalls who inflicted further defeat upon them at Dalry near Tyndrum. The course of Bruce's flight through the later autumn and winter is uncertain, but assuredly included Kintyre, Rathlin and the Hebrides where he found sanctuary with Angus Og MacDonald and support from Christiana MacRuari which enabled him to slip past the English blockade and into his home territory of Carrick.

By the time of his reappearance in the spring of 1307, the Bruce's fortunes were rising into the ascendant when in May he was able to defeat an English army in Ayrshire and less than two months later Edward I was dead. At which point, King Robert turned from his English to his Scottish enemies, namely the Balliol-Comyn faction and including the MacDougalls with whom he had a number of scores to settle. Alexander MacDougall's son John – known in the genealogies as *Eoin Bacach* or 'John the Lame' – had probably taken the place of his elderly father in command of the MacDougall forces at Dalry. John Bacach is said by Barbour's fourteenth-century verse history of *The Bruce* to have hunted the fugitive king with bloodhounds through the wilds of Ayrshire early in 1307 and is known to have been commissioned and funded by the English to guard Ayr with more than eight hundred troops in the July of that year. In the summer of 1308, however, he was watching from a galley while his warriors were driven down the slopes of Ben Cruachan to defeat at the hands of the Bruce's army before making his own escape seawards down Loch Etive.

It should be said that the chronology of King Robert's campaigns in Argyll is left unclear by the sources and has been variously interpreted by modern historians, but the sequence of events recently proposed by R. Andrew McDonald makes more than enough sense of inconsistent evidence to provide a workable scenario here.[62] Having inflicted decisive defeat on the Comyns at Inverurie in May 1308, the Bruce would have been well-placed to invade Argyll by the later summer, and so it was probably in

August that his forces advanced towards the MacDougall stronghold of Dunstaffnage. The detailed account of the ensuing conflict preserved in Barbour's poem tells how John MacDougall had placed his men on Ben Cruachan from where they would have rolled an avalanche of boulders down onto the invading forces had not lightly-armed warriors been sent ahead of the Bruce's army to take up position above the men of Argyll waiting in ambush. So it was that the MacDougall forces were trapped between the advancing army beneath them and a surprise attack from the slopes above. Their defeat was assured, and in its wake Alexander was forced into submission to King Robert, while his son John disappeared by sea and out of the historical record until the next year when he wrote to Edward II claiming to have arranged some form of truce with the Bruce.

Meanwhile, his father is on record as attending the Bruce's parliament in March 1309 (although quite possibly as a hostage in the king's custody) but neither his submission nor his son's truce were to outlast the summer, because King Robert was assembling a fleet on Loch Broom in August and in October was issuing a charter from Dunstaffnage. The conjunction of those dates confirmed by state papers taken together with the reference in Fordun's history to the fall of the MacDougall stronghold after a short siege indicates the sequence of events which drove Alexander and his son out of Scotland and brought them to Ireland by the early December of 1309. So it was that their heartland in Argyll, inherited by Dugall the name-giver from his father Somerled, was forfeited and soon afterwards passed to the Campbells, consigning the subsequent history of Alexander and his son to references in the English state papers.

Alexander himself was to survive the fall of Dunstaffnage by little more than a year, living out most of that time at Carlisle and at the English king's expense but apparently in ill health on the evidence of payment made in July 1310 to a man identified as his physician. Payments for the main-tenance of Alexander and his son had been ordered from officials in York on 1st April that year, but of greater significance here are the series of instructions to the treasurer of Ireland to pay sums of a hundred pounds for the support of Alexander's troops in Ireland. One such payment was authorised in April 1310 and another the following January, by which time Alexander of Argyll was evidently dead because this payment was made to his son who had taken command of his father's men in Ireland. In March 1311 Edward II gave John MacDougall a manor in Yorkshire for his support and in July commissioned him as 'Admiral and Captain of our fleet of ships' with orders to pursue the king's enemies in the Hebrides and along the coast of Argyll.

In March 1314, John was sent to Ireland on the king's business. He was there also in January of the following year when Edward is on record expressing sympathy for 'the losses and suffering of John of Argyll, now dwelling in Ireland, at the hands of the Scottish rebels' and instructing the Irish treasurer to make provision for him and his family. Another instruction to the treasurer to make good John's losses and maintain his men was issued after he had driven the Scots from the Isle of Man in February 1315, in which month he had also captured rebels off the Scottish coast whom the king commanded to be brought to Dublin. John Bacach was still in Dublin in September of that year, when he was waiting for naval reinforcements and urging payment of wages for his own men, but in May 1316 he had returned 'impotent in body' to London and been granted payment for his own and his family's maintenance. All of which evidence denies Barbour's claim for John's capture by the Bruce in 1315 and his subsequent death as a prisoner at Loch Leven, especially when a more reliable obituary is preserved in the English record of his dying whilst on pilgrimage to Canterbury in September 1317.

Between the death of John MacDougall in 1317 and the first notice of 'MacDowell the Galloglach' in the Irish annals at 1377 lies a span of six decades throughout which the historical record can supply no fragment of evidence which forges a link between the two. Tentative speculation, then, will have to suggest as much as it is able, and its starting-point might be recollection of the military entourage supported in Ireland by John Bacach – and, at least nominally, by his father before him – between 1310 and his departure for England towards the end of 1315 or in the first months of the following year.

Those forces are known only from the record of payments made by the English treasurer to John and his father for their support, but there is little doubt that a hundred pounds paid twice yearly would have financed a substantial body of men in early fourteenth-century Ireland. These warriors can be assumed to have been of West Highland origin and also of MacDougall association which, in at least some cases, would have been of an extended kinship character. They could, in fact, be most conveniently described (although in a form I usually avoid) as 'MacDougall clansmen', of whom those who had survived a decade of service under John of Argyll's command would have been veterans of the conflicts at Dalry, on Ben Cruachan and assuredly elsewhere besides. They would thus have been battle-hardened fighting-men of a quality comparable to that of the 'galloglas' brought to Ireland by Robert the Bruce when he came to the support of his brother Edward's invasion in 1316.

When John Bacach departed for England, the forces under his command in Ireland would have been left leaderless and, perhaps more importantly, without pay. Indeed, they may also have been owed arrears in view of John's demanding money for their wages from Edward II in the autumn of 1315, by which time, of course, the Bruce invasion of Ireland was already underway, and its early successes undoubtedly raising tensions in Dublin and the Pale (where the arrival in arms of the brother of his great enemy may even have played its part in prompting John Bacach's departure from Ireland). It is possible that such warriors as John had left in Dublin would have been gratefully recruited into the forces of the justiciar or his allied Anglo-Norman lords, but no less likely that Scottish fighting-men, especially ones of Gaelic background and character, might have been thought less than trustworthy for such service. Indeed, and for those same reasons, they may even have been expelled from the Pale, but if so there would have been ample opportunity for their employment elsewhere in Ireland where the demand for West Highland mercenary warriors was soon to become almost insatiable.

The absence of annal references to galloglas by any form of the name MacDougall through another two generations might be simply explained, then, by the recruitment of John Bacach's warriors into mercenary companies under the command of constables of other kindreds. In which case it is unlikely that the annalists would have had occasion to identify individuals of their name – at least until the year 1377 when 'MacDowell the Galloglach' is named among those slain in the defeat of the MacWilliam Burke and the O'Kelly by the O'Connors at Roscommon.[63]

The line of descent from John Bacach continued through his son Alan to his grandson and namesake, the John who had returned to Scotland with Edward Balliol by 1338 and was granted lands in Argyll (although only a portion of the former MacDougall holdings) by David II, son of Robert the Bruce. This later John of Lorn is best known to history from an indenture of September 1354 swearing brotherhood between himself and John of Islay, first Lord of the Isles, but after him the family in Scotland appears to have died out in the male line. In the genealogies preserved in MS 1467 and the *Book of Lecan*, however, four other lines of descent from Duncan, son of the eponymous Dugall, are grouped together as the 'Clan of John Bacach' (*Clann Eoin Bogaig*),[64] which would suggest these second cousins having formed an extended family which accompanied John Bacach from Argyll to Ireland if not also to England.

From which it might be reasonable to suggest the man called 'MacDowell the Galloglach' by the annalists as a descendant of one of the branches of the 'Clan of John Bacach'. The reappearance of one or more of those families as galloglas in Ireland around the time of John's own grandson's return to Scotland would well correspond to the annal notice of one of their senior members – or, more probably, a son of the same – slain in battle in Roscommon in 1377. The first MacDowell more properly identified in the annals is an Alexander who was in command of the 'Clann Dowell' with the O'Kellys when they were defeated by the MacSweeney galloglas of the Clanricard Burkes in the battle of Bel Atha Lige in Galway in 1419. The terms in which the Connacht annalist records his death bear fulsome testimony to his great reputation as a warrior:

> However, that doughty champion never before overcome in battle or combat or onset, Alexander MacDowell, was killed there with his followers and two sons.

Having confirmed his military prowess, it is unfortunately not possible to trace the descent of the formidable Alexander, because only one of the pedigrees of the 'Clan of John Bacach' extends further than John's own generation (but with only four names in two generations, none of which recur among MacDowell galloglas identified in the annals). Nor can the name Alexander, which occurs in such profusion throughout the MacDougall genealogies, offer any further precise indication of this Alexander's descent.

It may have been that Alexander's line was extinguished when his sons were slain beside him in 1419, because when the name MacDowell next appears – in the *Annals of Connacht* at 1462 – it is borne by a Turlough, constable to the MacRannell in Leitrim, who was taken prisoner in a contention between rival MacRannell factions. It is quite possible that this Turlough represented another line of the MacDowells, because there is evidence to suggest different branches of the kindred by the second half of the fifteenth century, principally the notice of a Ewen MacDowell 'treacherously slain in his own house by the sons of Colla MacDowell' entered in the *Annals of Connacht* at 1469 where the culprits are styled as the 'Clann Colla'. Another entry by the same annalist at 1471 offers evidence for MacDowell galloglas on freelance mercenary service when it notices William, son of Colla MacDowell (and thus also of the 'Clann Colla'), slain 'as he was returning home from the Leinster service'. Freelance mercenary activity in Leinster would suggest an association of the Mac-Dowells with the MacDonnell galloglas of that province, which may hark back to 1419 when Alexander MacDowell and his sons were fighting beside the MacDonnells of Connacht at the battle of Bel Atha Lige.

The given name of William might be taken to indicate his being the son of an Anglo-Irish mother, as indeed could that of the Walter who was one of the two MacDowells in the service of the MacRannell mentioned by annal entries of another internecine clash in 1473. The second of those MacDowells was Donough, son of Turlough, who reappears in the service of the MacDermots of Moylurg when he was taken prisoner by an O'Connor raid on Roscommon in 1490. Thirty years later MacDowells were still in the service of the MacDermots on the evidence of Gilladuff (son of the William killed in 1471) who is styled 'constable of Moylurg' by the Connacht annalist's entry of his obituary at 1520.

By the sixteenth century MacDowell galloglas are found almost nowhere other than Roscommon, the territory most closely associated with the kindred, but the annal record of individually-named MacDowell galloglas has expired before 1530, presumably again as a result of the death in battle of hereditary constables who left no able successors. The very last reference to MacDowell galloglas is found in the *Annals of the Four Masters* at 1570 and mentions 'a battle of the galloglas of the Clan Dowell' serving – apparently beside the Leinster MacDonnells – in the President of Connacht's forces at the battle of Shrule.

For all the various difficulties involved in following the descent of the MacDowells, at least their patronymic can be traced back to a genuinely historical eponymous ancestor. So too can those of the MacSweeneys, MacDonnells, and MacRorys, and even the MacSheehys can claim descent from an historical name-giver who is plausibly identified by a reliable source of Clan Donald tradition. The same cannot be said for the last of the six galloglas kindreds, because nowhere in Scotland or Ireland is there any historical record of an ancestor known by the personal name *Cába*.

Clann Cába – The MacCabes

The first reference to any member of the MacCabe galloglas kindred is found in the *Annals of the Four Masters* at the year 1358 where an *Aédh Mac Cába* is named among the slain when the O'Neill won 'a victory . . . over the people of Oriel and Fermanagh'.

Neither the Four Masters nor the Connacht annalist (who makes a similar entry at the same date) present *Mac Cába* as other than a customary patronymic form of surname, and yet *Cába* is unknown as a Gaelic personal name in Ireland or in Scotland. Thus there would seem to have been no eponymous ancestor from whom the MacCabes' descent might be claimed, which led Patrick Woulfe – in his reference work on Irish names – to the conclusion that 'son of Cába [is] probably a nickname'. Having confirmed the MacCabes as 'a military family of Norse origin who came over from the Hebrides in the fourteenth century',[65] he looked for the origin of their nickname in the Irish term for 'a cap or hood', but there is another – and perhaps more likely – possibility in the Scottish Gaelic noun *cabar*. Its meaning of 'a pole or roof-beam' is so obviously evocative of the long-handled axe which represented the characteristic galloglas weapon as to suggest 'sons of the pole [-axe]' as an especially fitting *nom de guerre* for a mercenary warrior family.

While the Irish recognition of the MacCabes as a galloglas kindred can be taken as conclusive evidence for their Scottish origin, the name itself supplies no indication of their parent lineage. In fact, the only such indication is found in old Irish genealogies, notably the collection compiled in the seventeenth century by Duald MacFirbis which includes a short pedigree of *Clann Cába* descending the kindred from 'Tormod, who was called MacCaba; son of Constantine Caomh of Innsi Breatan'. John O'Donovan, editor of the *Annals of the Four Masters*, pursued the question in the 1860s when he compared the MacFirbis genealogy of the MacCabes with that of the MacLeods and found the same 'Tormod, son of Constantine' occurring in both pedigrees, thus indicating the MacCabes as an offshoot of the MacLeods of the Western Isles. Further support for that proposal is supplied by the MacCabe genealogy when it associates a son of Tormod with what can only be a garbled form of the Scottish Gaelic place-name *na-Hearadh*, which would point more specifically to the descent of the MacCabe galloglas kindred from a branch of the MacLeods of Harris who are known in the Gaelic as the *Siol Tormoid*.[66]

As the last of the line of hereditary genealogists and historians of Lecan in Sligo, Duald MacFirbis represents an authority of stature and his work is thought to preserve material bearing on Scottish and Irish families of Norse descent which has been long since lost. It should be said, though, that his genealogy of the MacLeods cannot be considered impeccably historical when – as in other old Irish pedigrees of families whose origin lay outwith Ireland – names from myth and legend obviously fill gaps between and beyond names preserved by authentic tradition. Even so, the claim for the MacCabes' descent from the MacLeods, which is also supported by old Fermanagh genealogies, represents the only evidence for the origin of this most enigmatic of the galloglas kindreds and, for all the dubious detail of its earlier generations, can still be considered perfectly feasible.

The tradition of the MacLeods has always shown great pride in their Norse ancestry, and with some justice when recent research has traced them back through a sister of Godred Crovan, founding dynast of the royal house of Man, to the celebrated Olaf Cuaran, who was king of Dublin in the later tenth century.[67] The name MacLeod, however, does not make its first appearance in the formal historical record until 1343, the year assigned to the charters by which David II granted lands in Glenelg to a Malcolm MacLeod, son of Tormod, and in Assynt to Malcolm's nephew Torquil (for whom are named the *Siol Torcaill* MacLeods of Lewis).

When the first notice of a MacCabe in the Irish annals is found just fifteen years after the date of those charters, it is tempting to identify the Tormod of the MacFirbis genealogy with the Tormod known in the charter as the father of Malcolm MacLeod. Indeed, a rough calculation of generations back from the Enri MacCabe, son of Gillachrist, son of Flaherty, who is included in the MacFirbis pedigree and whose obituary is entered in three sets of Irish annals at the year 1460, would make the two Tormods approximate contemporaries. They might thus be proposed as one and the same – were it not for Tormod, father of Malcolm, being the son of the eponymous Leod, whose name may represent a gaelicised form of the Norse *Ljot* but can hardly be recognised in the 'Constantine Caomh' claimed by the Irish pedigree as the father of 'Tormod, who was called MacCaba'. 'Constantine', however, is a name so uncharacteristic of Gaelic-Norse pedigrees as to be discounted as an invention of the Irish genealogies,[68] so the eponym of the MacCabes might still be plausibly identified if not as Tormod MacLeod himself, quite possibly as a brother or half-brother with the same given name and for that reason called by a cognomen (something not unknown among Gaelic families even in relatively recent times).

While the MacLeods of Harris and Lewis are descended from a branch of the Norse of Man associated with and settled in the Outer Hebrides for some generations by the fourteenth century, there is insufficient detail on record even to guess at the circumstances which brought about the relocation of the MacCabe branch to Ireland. Even so, just one clue may be found in the annal entry at 1358 where the annalist makes an association of Aedh MacCabe with 'the people of Oriel and Fermanagh'. The name of Oriel (now County Monaghan) derives from the tribes known as the *Airgialla* who first emerged in the fifth century as allies of the Ui Neill in their conquest of Ulster. The hostility engendered between the Airgialla and the original Ulstermen (the *Uladh*) in that ancient conflict may well have endured over the centuries to shape alliances when the interest of the Norse of Dublin in the northern coast of Ireland brought them into conflict with the descendants of the Uladh in Antrim. As I have suggested elsewhere and in an eleventh-century context,[69] such a situation would have provided a likely basis for some form of alliance between the Dublin Norse and the tribes of the Airgialla, a relationship which could well have continued into the fourteenth century when the 'people of Oriel and Fermanagh' found themselves in need of Hebridean fighting-men for service as their galloglas. By which time descendants of the Dublin Norse had been long established at the northernmost extent of the old Manx 'kingdom of the Isles' where they were soon to reappear in the historical record as the MacLeods of the Outer Hebrides; and it seems fully probable that it was to them that the descendants of the Airgialla might have looked to recruit their galloglas.

However the MacCabe galloglas were first brought to Ireland, the geography of their arrival and expansion there followed a pattern unlike that of other galloglas kindreds. Their first appearance in the annal record at 1358 associates one of their name with Oriel, where they were firmly established by the last decade of the fourteenth century on the evidence of the Bryan MacCabe, who is styled 'constable of the galloglas of the country of Oriel' by his obituary entered in the *Annals of Ulster* at 1394. He would thus have been constable to the MacMahons of that country, and the Tomas MacCabe who accompanied Philip MacMahon when he came to Dundalk to pay homage to Richard II in the following year was assuredly Bryan's successor, and very probably his son. The official record of the submissions also supplies evidence for the more specific location of the kindred when it identifies Tomas as 'MacCabe of Clogher diocese'.

Some ten years earlier, however, an entry in the *Annals of the Four Masters* at 1386 offers the first indication of the kindred's expansion beyond Oriel and Fermanagh into neighbouring Breifne when it notices a Donough MacCabe 'slain by Manus O'Reilly'. Even without any further detail of circumstances, the entry might be taken to suggest this Donough as the first of generations of MacCabe galloglas associated with the O'Reillys of east Breifne (now County Cavan) through the following two centuries. If he had somehow come awry with his employer and suffered the fatal consequence, it may have encouraged his son to seek service elsewhere, because the same annalists notice a 'son of Donough MacCabe' with the O'Donnells when he was killed at Farsetmore in Donegal some six years later. It is otherwise possible that Donough had been with the O'Rourkes of west Breifne (now County Leitrim) who were not infrequently at odds with the neighbouring O'Reillys. A branch of the kindred are known to have entered service with the O'Rourkes by 1416, in which year the *Annals of Ulster* record an incursion to the west of Upper Lough Erne and make reference to MacCabes as 'their [the O'Rourkes'] retained galloglas'.

MacCabe galloglas were certainly in the service of the O'Reillys by the early years of the fifteenth century when they were taking an active part in hostilities against the O'Rourkes, and the entry in the *Annals of Connacht* at 1402 might be read to suggest the duties of their service having extended to assassination:

> Fergal, son of Aed O'Rourke, son of the king of Breifne and a prince eligible for the kingship, was treacherously killed in his own house by Loughlin (*Lochlainn*) Calach MacCabe a fortnight before Easter. He was buried in the monastery of Sligo.

Open conflict between the two Breifnes had broken out by the following year, its cause said by the Connacht annalist to have been the capture of two young nobles of the O'Rourkes – and the wounding of one of them – by the O'Reillys. Little other detail of this 'war' is disclosed, other than a notice of 'Mahon, son of Gillachrist, son of Flaherty MacCabe . . . wounded by O'Rourke's men'.

Employment by the O'Reillys would seem not to have precluded the

MacCabes from freelance enterprise, because the same Loughlin Calach mentioned at 1402 is noticed by the same annalist three years later, but on this occasion accompanying the MacDermot of Moylurg on a circuit of Roscommon in demand of tribute. MacDermot met with a hostile reception and had need of 'the support of Donough Mor MacDonnell his constable, Loughlin Calach MacCabe and all the new levies of Moylurg [who] made great slaughter of the rabble'. The reference to 'the new levies of Moylurg' would indicate Loughlin Calach among additional galloglas specially re-cruited by the MacDermot for a contentious mission, because Loughlin was back again in the service of the O'Reilly when he was killed beside his brother on the raiding expedition noticed by the Four Masters at 1413:

> Tomas Og O'Reilly and the MacCabes (*Clann Cába*) went on an incursion into Meath and committed acts of conflagration and depredation there. The English overtook them and Mahon Mac-Cabe, Loughlin MacCabe, and a great number of their people were slain.

Although the entry does not mention their relationship, the Mahon MacCabe slain beside Loughlin was almost certainly his brother when both are identified elsewhere in the annals as sons of Gillachrist, son of Flaherty. Mahon himself was evidently the father of six sons who followed him into the profession of arms.

The Four Masters record an internecine conflict between MacRannells in 1433 when one faction 'took the sons of Mahon MacCabe into their pay to assist them' on an incursion into the Moy south of Lough Finvoy in Leitrim. After burning a township, the raiders withdrew . . .

> But on leaving the town they were overtaken by a strong body of troops; and the sons of Mahon being in the rearguard, three of them, Ross, Donough, and Bryan, were slain on the spot together with many others. Rory, their eldest brother, was taken prisoner and he half dead; but Turlough, who was the fifth son and whose mother was Una, daughter of Sean O'Reilly, escaped.

A sixth brother, who is identified by the Four Masters as 'Ewen Caech, son of Mahon MacCabe' in their notice of his death in battle beside the O'Reilly in 1460, had evidently been constable to the O'Reilly because the annal entry concludes with the statement that 'Cathal, son of Ewen, assumed his [father's] place'.

It is likely that Ewen, and probably one of his brothers before him, had followed their uncle Enri into that same office of constable on the evidence of Enri's obituary entered by the annalists also at the year 1460. This Enri is listed in the MacFirbis pedigree which indicates his descent through the senior line of the family, but is scarcely noticed by the annal record although he apparently survived to die of natural causes at an advanced age. Enri was probably succeeded as constable by his nephew(s) following his retirement from office by reason of age, but his high status is strongly implied by the entry of his obituary in similar detail by three sets of annals, of which the *Annals of the Four Masters* offers a typical example:[70]

> Enri, son of Gillachrist MacCabe, went with O'Farrell into the Annaly [now County Longford], where he died of a short sickness at Lissardowlin. He was carried to Cavan to be interred there, attended by two hundred and eighty galloglas armed with axes.

The close association of this line of the MacCabes with the O'Reillys may have been underwritten by marriage when the mother of one of the sons of Mahon is identified by the Four Masters as 'Una, daughter of Sean O'Reilly'. Nonetheless, their constables and galloglas appear to have been regularly available for recruitment in a freelance capacity and there is no indication of their having formed any exclusive bond resembling that of the MacSweeney Fanad with the O'Donnell.

What is known of the MacCabes, then, indicates a pattern distinctly different from that found in the histories of other galloglas kindreds who first appear in the north of Ireland, expanding afterwards through Connacht down into Munster as they are drawn into the service of Anglo-Irish magnates. Even the MacDonnells of Leinster, who represent something of an exception in moving eastward and into the service of the English crown, found their way there out of Connacht.

The MacCabes, however, are rarely found outwith the Irish midlands, specifically the territory contained within the modern counties of Monaghan, Fermanagh, Cavan and Leitrim. They first appear in Oriel and Fermanagh, as constables to the MacMahons of Oriel by the end of the fourteenth century and afterwards with the O'Reillys in Cavan and the O'Rourkes in Leitrim, which suggests successive generations extending themselves out of Oriel into the service of neighbouring chieftains. Annal references associate MacCabes with the Maguires of Fermanagh in the sixteenth century, and their earlier presence in that country is confirmed by the MacCabe pedigrees included in the Fermanagh genealogies. There is a curious reference to a Melaghlin MacCabe as 'constable of the two Breifnes, and also of Fermanagh and Oriel' in his obituary entered by the Four Masters at 1424, which is echoed by the same annalists' obituary of his son Maine entered at 1455 where they describe him as the *adhbhar* (or 'heir') 'of a constable of the two Breifnes, of Oriel and of Fermanagh', which Dr Simms has suggested as evidence that 'one military family might supply mercenary captains to several independent Irish lordships'.[71] What is certainly true is that the four territories named by those two entries encompass the principal orbit of the MacCabes' galloglas activity and, for whatever reason, they had no need or inclination to extend themselves outwith the midland region.

The most prominent of the galloglas kindreds – namely the MacSweeneys and MacDonnells – were those who extended themselves most widely across Ireland. Their introduction in the thirteenth century seems to have been associated in some wise with marriage alliances between powerful families in Ulster and the West Highlands. The MacCabes, by contrast, were unknown by that name in Scotland and made their first appearance in Oriel and Fermanagh where the principal families had maintained little if any recorded contact with the nobility of the West Highlands since the end of the eleventh century.[72] The circumstances indicated by their first notice in the annals suggest that increasing pressure on Oriel and Fermanagh from the resurgent O'Neills might have created the need for the MacMahons and Maguires to recruit their own galloglas. Thereafter, the MacCabes extended themselves into Breifne but apparently no further to the south or west and so were not drawn into those regions where they might have entered the service of the Anglo-Irish lords.

In the last analysis, then, the different course of the history of the MacCabes is probably attributable to their lesser numbers and to the relatively late date of their arrival in Ireland, because by that point in the fourteenth century the galloglas phenomenon was approaching the critical point of its evolution from a Scottish luxury import into an Irish military institution.

III

WARRIORS

'Those that do not lightly abandon the field,
but byde the brunt to the death'

While the Irish annals represent the principal source of information for the emergence and expansion of the galloglas kindreds in medieval Ireland, they are rather less helpful in the realm of their strictly military history. It is true that the annalists regularly record the names of constables and the numbers of men under their command slain in action, and that their accounts of the heat of battle, even if suspiciously formulaic on occasion, can still offer some genuinely evocative colour. It is also true that they make passing references to weaponry and tactics from which historians have been able to draw wider inferences, but nowhere in the annal record is there found any description in detail of the appearance, equipment and organisation which made the galloglas so prominent a presence in medieval Irish warfare.

Consequently, very much of what is known of the galloglas as warriors is greatly dependent upon the testimony of English observers informed by first-hand experience of Ireland in the sixteenth century. Some of these were themselves soldiers, while others were state officials or simply settlers, but all had played some part in the Tudor re-conquest of Ireland and so could hardly be expected to appreciate the culture and custom of the 'wild Irish'. When writing of the galloglas, however, all seem to share at least something of the 'wonderment' with which Elizabethan courtiers followed Shane O'Neill's bodyguard in London in 1562. As does Sir Anthony Sentleger, Lord Deputy of Ireland, in his report on Irish soldiery made to Henry VIII in 1543, where he points out the characteristic weapon of the galloglas and pays impressive tribute to their warrior ethos:

> As to their footmen, they have one sort, which be harnessed in mayle
> and bassinettes, having every one of them his weapon, called a sparre,
> much like the axe of the Tower, and they be named galloglasse . . .
> these sort of men be those that do not lightly abandon the field, but
> byde the brunt to the death.[1]

John Dymmok's *Treatise of Ireland* was written more than fifty years after Sentleger's dispatch, and rather less is known of its author, except that he was in attendance upon the Earl of Essex, Elizabeth's Lord Lieutenant in Ireland in the last years of the sixteenth century. Nonetheless, it is Dymmok's account which preserves an exceptional wealth of detail in its description of galloglas as

> . . . picked and selected men of great and mighty bodies, cruel without compassion. The greatest force of the battle consisteth in them, choosing rather to die than to yield; so that when it cometh to hardy blows, they are quickly slain, or win the field. They are armed with a shirt of mail, a skul, and a skeine: the weapon they most use is a battle-axe or halbert, six feet long, the blade whereof is somewhat like a shoemaker's knife, and without a [s]pike; the stroke whereof is deadly where it lighteth. And being thus armed, reckoning to him a man for his harness bearer and a boy to carry his provisions, he is named a sparre, of his weapon so called, eighty of which sparres make a battle of galloglas.[2]

The galloglach's axe – which both Dymmok and Sentleger call his 'sparre' – would seem to have attracted the notice of every contemporary English writer on the subject. The Elizabethan poet Edmund Spenser, for example, lived for a time in County Cork and so was probably thinking of a MacSheehy when he described a galloglach 'armed in a long shirt of mail down to the calf of the leg, with a long broad axe in his hand'.[3]

'Commonly armed with a Scull, a shirt of mail, and a Galloglas Axe' is the very similar description supplied by Barnaby Rich, who appears the least impressed of all his contemporaries by the galloglach in action when he expressed the view that 'his service in the field is neither good against horsemen, nor able to endure an encounter of pikes, yet the Irish do make great account of them'.[4] It should be said that Rich himself fought as a pikeman at Monasternenagh in 1579 where his first experience of warfare in Ireland was to watch MacSheehys of the Desmond galloglas 'throw themselves screaming over the English pikes until the pikemen's hands ran red with blood', and yet his view of their quality was not shared by Sir William Stanley who fought in another part of the same field. While Rich considered the battle a triumph for the English forces, Stanley felt they had narrowly escaped defeat and said of the galloglas onslaught that 'these rebels came as resolutely to fight as the best soldiers in Europe'.[5]

Nor was the fascination with axes restricted to English-born observers when it was evidently shared by Richard Stanyhurst, the Oxford-educated son of a prominent Dublin family and contributor of most of the Irish material to Holinshed's *Chronicle*:

> Their weapons [i.e. the blades thereof] are one foot in length, resembling double-bladed hatchets, almost sharper than razors, fixed on shafts of more than ordinary length, with which when they strike they inflict a dreadful wound.

Stanyhurst's account corroborates those of Sentleger and Dymmok when he describes

> . . . men of great stature, of more than ordinary strength of limb, powerful swordsmen, but, at the same time, altogether sanguinary and by no means inclined to give quarter . . . In every sharp and severe engagement, should they come to close fighting, they either soon kill, or are killed.[6]

Taken together with Camden's description of Shane O'Neill's escort in London, these accounts provide a remarkably detailed portrait of the galloglach as he appeared to sixteenth-century English observers: a man of exceptional strength and stature, wearing a shirt of chain-mail over another of saffron-dyed linen, and on his head an open-faced iron or leather helmet – the same type called a 'bassinette' (properly *bascinet*) by Sentleger and a 'skul' by Dymmok and Rich – fitted with a mail cowl (or *pisane*) protecting the neck and shoulders. The long-handled battle-axe is consistently singled out as his characteristic weapon, although the discrepancy in the descriptions offered by Sentleger and Dymmok is taken to indicate more than one type of blade in use. Dymmok also mentions a knife which he calls a 'skeine' (from the Gaelic *sgian*) while Stanyhurst and others confirm the galloglas having also fought with a sword, perhaps in some cases of the two-handed type.

Sentleger appears to include 'darts' (or light throwing spears akin to javelins) in the galloglas armoury, although such weapons are more usually associated with the lightly-armed kern. In fact, Sentleger is not entirely clear whether he means this weapon used by the galloglach himself or by one of his attendants when he states that 'their boys bear for them three darts apiece, which darts they throw as they come to the hand stripe [close combat]'. These 'boys' are more precisely distinguished by Dymmok as 'a man for his harness bearer and a boy to carry his provisions', the term 'harness' being used in its sixteenth-century meaning of battle-gear. An official account of 'the power of Irishmen', compiled around 1534, specifies each galloglach to have been accompanied 'with one knave to bear his harness, whereof some have spears, some have bows',[7] which would suggest that it was the harness-bearer who went with his master into action using darts as his own weapon. Andrew McKerral, however, suggests a convincing distinction (and one which may have been easily overlooked by Sentleger) between the kern's dart and the 'short heavy spear used as a missile' which he recognises as an earlier 'Viking weapon' very plausibly inherited by the galloglas from their Norse ancestors.[8]

The same report is in approximate agreement with Dymmok's account of galloglas' fighting formation when it explains that 'a battle of galloglas be sixty or eighty men harnessed on foot with sparres, each with one knave to bear his harness'. Dymmok's version of the same formation also includes the 'boy to carry his provisions' as well as the harness-bearer and the galloglach himself in the fighting unit which he calls a 'sparre' (thus named for the axe in the same way as the individual member of a game shoot is referred to as 'a gun'). In fact, Dymmok's use of the term 'sparre' can be read as perfectly authentic because he was using the Middle English *sparre* (meaning 'spear') as the most convenient phonetic equivalent for the Irish *sparr* meaning a cross-beam or joist.[9]

There is good reason, then, to recognise *sparr* as the Gaelic name applied by the Irish to the long-handled axe and also, by obvious association, to the fighting unit comprising a galloglach thus equipped and with at least one supporting attendant in arms. The term 'battle', however, which was used by most English sources to indicate a formation of about eighty such units, is clearly of no such Gaelic origin. It was, in fact, the term generally applied by sixteenth-century English writers to any substantial formation of troops within an army, and so would have been quite naturally used by Dymmok and his contemporaries as their immediate equivalent of the Irish word *corrughadh* by which the annal record of the fifteenth century and later calls formations of galloglas.

Further light is thrown on the subject by an official record of the 'wages of Irish men of war' dated to April 1575 which explains how a 'captain of galloglas . . . in a band of a hundred hath to advance his wages, thirteen dead pays out of the hundred'. By which, of course, is meant that the constable could claim payment for more galloglas than were present under

(PLATE 1) Iron pole-axe head from Derryhollagh, Co. Antrim, dated to c.1300 or later and thought to have been an early galloglach weapon. (Photo: National Museum of Ireland)

The warrior grave-slabs at Saddell on Kintyre (PLATE 2) and at Kildalton on Islay (PLATE 3 on facing page) - dated to the 14th or early 15th centuries - offer closely contemporary evidence for the appearance of the earliest galloglas in Ireland. (Photos: Jenni Marsden)

(PLATE 4) Dating from the later 12th century, Castle Sween in Knapdale was named for - and presumably built by - the ancestor and eponym of the MacSweens of Knapdale and the MacSweeney galloglas kindred in Ireland. (Photo: Historic Scotland)

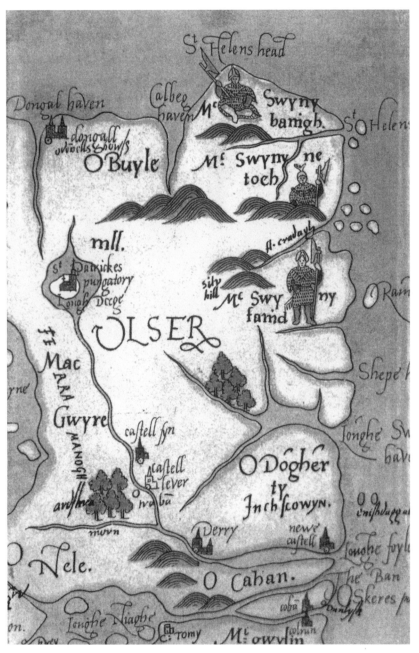

(PLATE 5) The MacSweeney territories of Fanad, na Tuath and Banagh are illustrated with sketches of galloglach figures in this detail from John Goghe's 1567 map of Ireland. (Reproduced by courtesy of the Council of Trustees of the National Library of Ireland)

Albrecht Dürer's drawing of 'war men of Ireland' dated to 1521 (PLATE 7 above) provides the most impressive contemporary portrait of galloglas with their armed attendants. (facsimile print, National Gallery of Ireland)

(PLATE 6 on facing page). Two of the figures from the late 15th-century carvings of galloglas decorating the 'O'Connor' tomb in Roscommon abbey. (Photo: Duchas, The Heritage Service)

(PLATE 8) The enigmatic warrior figure from the hunting scene carved above Alexander MacLeod's tomb of 1521 in St Clement's church at Rodel, Harris. (Photo: Royal Commission on the Ancient and Historical Monuments of Scotland)

his command and keep the difference for himself. 'So the band of a hundred is but eighty-seven men.'[10] Had the more creative constables got into the habit of claiming more 'dead pays' than the number nodded through by the official rules, it would explain how a 'battle' of galloglas came to represent some eighty – or even as few as sixty – fighting-men.

Such then, if only in summary, is the account preserved in the sixteenth-century English documentary record of the appearance and equipment of galloglas and it is helpfully – if, perhaps, unexpectedly – illustrated by a drawing by no less a master than Albrecht Dürer which shows a group of five figures, two of them identified by lines in the artist's hand as 'war men of Ireland beyond England'. One of these wears a peaked iron helmet and a mail shirt with a long knife at his belt, carrying a two-handed sword over his shoulder, a bow in his other hand and clutch of arrows under his arm. His companion wears a more compact form of helmet, a long pleated gown and carries a spear. Behind them stand the other three figures identified by another handwritten line as 'poor men of Ireland'. Two of these are of youthful appearance, wearing their hair cropped short in the neck but hanging long over the forehead in the traditional Irish 'glib' style and carrying long-shafted axes, while the third is a more obviously mature man wrapped in a cloak and clutching beneath it another two-handed sword.

There is no record of Dürer's having visited Ireland or any other part of the British Isles, and yet his 'war men' and 'poor men of Ireland' correspond so remarkably to the evidence of the documentary record that they can only be recognised as two galloglas accompanied by three armed attendants. It is possible that his finely-detailed drawing was an elaborated copy of a sketch made by someone else, although it is signed with his own monogram and dated 1521, in which year he is known to have been in the Low Countries, where he may well have seen some of the first Irish mercenaries to have found their way to the Continent and who would have supplied unusually interesting models for a group portrait.

Another three figure drawings placed as illustrative details on John Goghe's map of Ireland dated to 1567 are very much less accomplished in execution than Dürer's work, but of no less interest as portraits of galloglas dressed in long shirts of mail, wearing helmets of somewhat variant design, but wielding closely similar long-handled axes. The location of each figure in one of the three districts of Tyrconnell immediately associated with the principal septs of the MacSweeneys – and boldly labelled by the mapmaker as Banagh, na Tuath and Fanad – bears its own testimony to the characteristic appearance and armament of galloglas, as it does also to their prominence in Ireland, at the time the map was drawn.

The important question hanging over this evidence from the sixteenth century, of course, is to what extent it can be considered valid for the galloglas of earlier – and more properly 'medieval' – periods. The appearance, arms and armour of galloglas portrayed on stone carvings dated to the second half of the fifteenth century, principally those in Roscommon abbey and at Dungiven priory in County Derry, corresponds fairly closely to the descriptions by Tudor observers. Nor does it greatly differ from warrior carvings on West Highland grave slabs of the fourteenth century, and so there is good reason to believe there was much about the appearance of the élite professional fighting-men of the sixteenth century which would have been recognisable in their Hebridean and West Highland forebears on their earliest arrival in Ireland.

There are other characteristics noticed by sixteenth-century observers, however, which would not have been found among the first generations of MacSweeneys and MacDonnells settled in Donegal and Tyrone in the second half of the thirteenth century. While their weaponry and war-gear apparently remained largely unchanged into the 1580s, other aspects which so distinguished the galloglas can only be recognised as refinements and adaptations which had emerged in the course of their evolution into a distinctly Irish military phenomenon. These other, perhaps even more significant, features – such as their fighting techniques, battle tactics, military organisation, and mercenary warrior ethos – had probably begun to appear in the second half of the fourteenth century, but are not fully evident until the later decades of the century following, by which time the galloglas had extended themselves out of Ulster and through Connacht into Munster and into Leinster. What must have been meant by the annalist's first use of the term 'galloglas' in 1290 was simply Hebridean and West Highland warriors resident in Ireland – or, in fact, at that time principally in Ulster – and available for hire, and thus only the most embryonic form of the élite professional warrior class called by the same name when it was to be found in every Irish province two and three hundred years later.

No such warrior class had been known in Ireland – at least in historical times – before the emergence of the galloglas, even though mercenary fighting-men had, of necessity, been in ever wider use there since at least as early as the eve of the eleventh century. The provision for a muster of forces as set out in old Irish law tracts reflects the ritual, rather than properly military, character of warfare in Ireland before the Scandinavian impact. Aggressive warfare appears to have been organised around raiding for cattle (the principal form of wealth in early Ireland) and burning roof thatch rather than wholesale slaughter of an enemy, while set-piece battles seem to have been of a distinctly ritual character and sometimes focused on single combat between champions.

For the conduct of such warfare, a local king was empowered by social contract to summon his sub-chieftains and their followers to a hosting, and similarly authorised to distrain their property should they fail to respond. The same contract also imposed conditions on the king, requiring his cause for the hosting to be just and specifying not only the season but the territory over which it should extend. Warfare in early Ireland, then, was predominantly concerned with prestige and submission and generally conducted on a small scale. It was the occasional occupation – or even recreation – of young noblemen, usually mounted on horseback, and bearing the traditional weaponry of sword, spear and shield, but no realistic comparison to a professional warrior class. Nor did the traditional system of muster for war provide the king with a standing army, and the only semblance of such a permanent force mentioned in the law tracts was a group of four freed men called *amuis* (or 'hirelings') who stood around the king as his personal bodyguard at ale-feasts while two more bearing arms were on guard at the door of his hall. Dr Simms' detailed survey of the emergence of mercenary warriors in Ireland suggests such bodyguards would have been needed in greater numbers as provincial kingdoms came to extend over wider territories, and she points to evidence for a Cathal, son of Fogartach, who is styled *rí-amus* (effectively 'royal champion') by his obituary entered in the *Annals of Inisfallen* at 968. The same Cathal is mentioned also in the *Cogadh Gaedhel re Gallaibh* ('The Wars of the Irish with the Foreigners', written in the twelfth century), where he is described as 'commanding a hundred armed men fit for battle, each man of them having a large warrior's shield at his side'.[11]

The Scandinavian impact provided the initial impetus towards the militarisation of early medieval Ireland, and the process was already in train by the time Brian Boru first demonstrated the possibility of a realistic high-kingship in the dawn of the eleventh century. All those restraints set out in old law tracts rendered the traditional hosting quite inadequate for the purposes of those who sought to follow Brian's example, and so the twelfth century saw the more ambitious Irish kings hiring the most effective mercenary forces available from wherever they could find them. The Dublin Norse had long offered a source of mercenary warriors. So too did the Gaelic Norse of Argyll and the Irish Sea zone on the evidence of an entry in the *Annals of the Four Masters* at 1154, in which year Turlough O'Connor, who claimed high-kingship of Ireland, despatched a fleet out of Connacht to plunder Tyrconnell and Inishowen. The king of Ailech sent emissaries 'across the sea . . .'

> and hired the ships of Galloway, Arran, Kintyre, Man and the shores
> of Scotland also. And when they had come near to Inishowen, they
> collided with the other fleet. A sea battle was fought between them,
> terribly and stubbornly. They fought from prime till none [i.e. before
> 7 a.m. until after 2 p.m.]; and a great many Connachtmen were killed
> by the *gaill,* [until] the host of the *gaill* was routed with slaughter.

There would have been nothing so very unusual, then, in the Leinster king Dermot MacMurrough's looking to hire military assistance from Norman Wales against another O'Connor high-king in 1176. He was neither the first nor the last Irish lord to employ Norman mercenaries, but the great difference in Dermot's case, of course, lay in the ultimate price of his imported knights having been the Anglo-Norman conquest of Ireland.

It was the subsequent Norman impact which was to greatly advance the militarisation of Irish society, and with it the more widespread use of mercenaries. While there is a claim in the *Cogadh* that Munstermen hired themselves out to fight for Ui Neill kings of the north before the rise of Brian Boru, the true native Irish mercenary warrior is not to be found in the sources until the late thirteenth century when official records begin to mention 'kern'. Derived from the Irish term *ceithearn*, simply meaning a 'warband', the term is used to identify a warrior type which had been known in Ireland at least a hundred years earlier and was still to feature prominently in accounts of Irish soldiery from the second half of the sixteenth century. Sir Anthony Sentleger's description of kern, in his dispatch of 1543, as 'naked men, but only [i.e. except for] their shorts and small coats', armed with 'darts and short bows',[12] bears the most extraordinary similarity to the words of the Norman churchman Gerald of Wales when he wrote in 1185 of Irish warriors who 'go naked and

unarm[our]ed into battle [with] short spears and two darts'.[13] The armament of the kern in the twelfth century would seem then to have been little
changed even into the later sixteenth century when John Dymmok
described him as

> . . . a kind of footman, slightly armed wth a sword, a target [small
> shield] of wood, or a bow and sheaf of arrows with barbed heads, or
> else three darts which they cast with a wonderful facility and nearness,
> a weapon more noisome to the enemy, especially horsemen, than it is
> deadly.[14]

Such basic weaponry was well enough suited to a cattle raid and guerilla
operations in wild terrain, especially when, as Sentleger admits, these kern
were accustomed to the rough and trackless country of 'woods and
morasses, in which they are hard to beaten'. No less valuable to an Irish
chieftain of the twelfth or thirteenth century, however, was their presence
as permanently armed fighting-men available for hire as and when they
were needed. Between such periods of employment, kern seem to have
been inclined to self-employment as brigands, which contributed to their
unsavoury reputation reflected in some of the Elizabethan accounts.
Stanyhurst, for example, compared them to 'rakehells, or the devil's black
guard, by reason of the stinking stir they keep where so ever they be.'[15]

Much semblance of military discipline, then, was hardly to be expected
of them, nor were they any better equipped to face Norman men-at-arms,
especially in open battle, than Irish horsemen – clutching light javelins and
riding without stirrups – could match Norman knights trained from youth
to fight on horseback with sword and lance. Set in that context, the
advantage of the galloglas becomes immediately apparent: fighting-men of
exceptional strength and stature armed and armoured as heavy infantry,
their discipline cemented by ancient bonds of kinship and their loyalty
ensured by the mercenary's wages, their professional ethos demanding
victory or death where they stood wielding war-axes capable of slicing off a
foeman's limb or cutting down a charging knight from the saddle of his
warhorse.

The problem with such a description is that it cannot have been what
was meant by the annalist's first reference to 'galloglas' at the year 1290. All
that can be inferred from that annal entry is warriors of the Clan Donald
having been brought to Ireland, probably in the entourage or as the dowry
of the O'Donnell's Scottish wife much like those who had accompanied

Aodh O'Connor's MacRuari bride to Derry in 1259. While less is known of how MacDonnells first came into the service of the O'Neills in Tyrone, it is clear that they were established there by the 1290s. Warriors of all of these aforementioned kindreds – and undoubtedly some MacSweeneys also – can thus be considered a familiar presence in the north of Ireland in the second half of the thirteenth century, and known as 'galloglas' by reason of their Hebridean and West Highland *gall-gaedhil* origin.

As to their specifically military role, it can hardly have been so very different – although probably somewhat aggrandised – from that of the bodyguards known in earlier times as *amuis*. In that same capacity of military escort to provincial kings, these first warriors called galloglas would undoubtedly have accompanied their employers on circuits of their countries, adding an extra dimension to whatever degree of intimidation was necessary to impose submission and extract tribute from sub-kings and vassal chieftains. In such a situation, of course, they could hardly not have been drawn into the action. On a cattle raid, to suggest just one likely example, they would have supplied the most effective rearguard as plundered livestock were driven off.

While some such warriors appear to have been retained in the service of one lord, there would seem to have been others, probably before the end of the thirteenth century and certainly by the second decade of the century following, who made themselves more widely available for hire as mercenaries. More reliable than bands of kern, but originally not so very unlike them, these may well have been what was meant by the annal reference to 'many other galloglas' who joined 'his mother's kin, the Clan Donald' to enable Turlough O'Donnell to depose his half-brother in 1290. Another, and perhaps better, example is found in the entry in the *Annals of Connacht* at 1316 when it tells how a 'daughter of Manus O'Connor hired a band of galloglas and gave them a reward for killing Rory, son of Donal O'Connor, so by them he was killed'.

Much though their role and character were to change from their earliest forms, galloglas continued to fulfil a bodyguard role even into the later sixteenth century, of which the MacSheehys who rescued their rebel earl of Desmond from capture by English troops in the 1580s are a good example, as indeed are the MacDonnells who formed Shane O'Neill's escort at Elizabeth's court some twenty years before. There is another – and unusually descriptive – reference to Shane's galloglas bodyguard in the *Annals of the Four Masters* at 1557. In that year, shortly before he succeeded his father as the O'Neill, Shane mustered forces to invade Tyrconnell in support for one of two rival sons of the O'Donnell, and the annalists tell how MacSweeney galloglas were sent to spy out O'Neill's forces encamped beside an arm of Lough Swilly not so far north of Raphoe. They came into the camp under cover of darkness and passed between shadows and flickering firelight 'until they came to the great central fire at the entrance to the son [i.e. Shane] of O'Neill's tent . . .'

> A huge torch, thicker than a man's body, was constantly flaming at a short distance from the fire, and sixty grim and redoubtable galloglas with sharp, keen axes, terrible and ready for action . . . were watching and guarding the son of O'Neill.

'Sharp, keen axes' again. By the mid-sixteenth century, the galloglach and his axe seem to have become as inseparable in the Irish as in the English sources, yet nowhere in the early annal record of galloglas is there any reference to battle-axes, and not until the last quarter of the fourteenth century is there any firm documentary association of the warrior with his characteristic weapon. In view of which, the galloglach's axe might serve as a useful index point with which to trace the evolution of the galloglas phenomenon and – for that reason among others – is worthy of consideration in some detail here.

There are known to have been axes of some sort in Ireland since Neolithic times, but they seem not to have been included with the sword and spear in the Irish armoury of the early historic Celtic period. The long-held, and assuredly accurate, belief is that it was the Norse who introduced the axe into Ireland as a formidable weapon of war. The Anglo-Norman churchman Gerald of Wales certainly believed so in the late twelfth century when he described the Irish armed with 'short spears, two darts and big axes well and carefully forged, which they have taken over from the Norwegians'.[16] The account of the battle of Clontarf in the *Cogadh* confirms axes having been used by Norse and by Irish (who, it should be said, fought on both sides of the conflict), when it describes Brian Boru slain by a chieftain of the Shetland Norse with 'a bright, gleaming, trusty battle-axe', and Irish warriors fighting with 'Lochlann [i.e. Norse] axes'.

The axe as weapon was also a Norse introduction into Scotland, where – as the modern authority on medieval Scottish weaponry, David Caldwell, confirms – 'many of those [axes] in use from the twelfth century onwards are derived from Viking types'.[17] To which might be added the reference in

Hakon's Saga to the Scots foot-soldiers attacking the Norwegians stranded at Largs in 1263 being armed with 'mostly bows and *spaurdur*', a term evidently indicating pole-weapons which A. O. Anderson translated as 'Irish axes'.[18] If only on the strength of that one fortunate item of contemporary evidence, there can be little doubt that at least some of the Gaelic-Norse fighting-men who appeared in Ireland out of Argyll and the Hebrides around much the same time would have been armed with just such a weapon. Those who followed in their wake through the following century are still more likely to have fought with axes on the evidence of John Barbour's *The Bruce*, where his account of the battle of Dalry in 1306 tells how John of Lorn's warriors . . .

> fought with their axes so fiercely,
> for they were one and all on foot,
> that they slew many of the [Bruce's] horse
> or to some gave great wounds.[19]

If those lines immediately invite comparison with galloglas engaging Anglo-Norman cavalry, it is worth remembering that Barbour was writing some seventy years after the event he describes, and so it is quite possible that his detail reflects the West Highland weaponry in use in his own time as distinct from that which inflicted defeat on the Bruce. While there is little, if any, evidence for the prominence of the axe in Scottish armouries of the Bruce period, there is a well-known image of a warrior bearing a long-shafted axe cut into a stone cross-shaft from the isle of Texa, off Islay, a carving firmly dated to the later fourteenth century and thus closely contemporary with Barbour's poem.

That same cross – inscribed, incidentally, with the name of Ranald (*Reginaldus*), son of the first Lord of the Isles and eponym of the Clanranald – is also closely contemporary with the first fully reliable reference in the Irish sources indicating a prominent association of galloglas with their axes. It is, in fact, the passage in the *Book of the MacSweeneys* earlier referred to here which sets out in some detail the terms under which Turlough Caoch of Fanad agreed to supply fighting-men to the O'Donnell:

And it was then that a levy of galloglas was made upon Clann Sweeney, and this is how the levy was made: two galloglas for each quarter of land, and two cows for each galloglach deficient, that is, one cow for the man himself and one for his equipment. And Clan

Sweeney say they are responsible for these as follows, that for each man equipped with a coat of mail and a breastplate, another should have a jack and a helmet;[20] that there should be no forfeit for a helmet deficient except the galloglach's brain (dashed out for want of it); and no fine for a missing axe except a shilling, nor for a spear, except a groat, which shilling and groat the constable should get, and the O'Donnell had no claim to make for either.

While the *Book of the MacSweeneys* is known to have been set down in the first half of the sixteenth century, its passage bearing on Turlough Caoch's contract reads as if in a different voice from that of the surrounding narrative, and so there is every likelihood of the scribe having transcribed the passage from a copy, if not the original, of a document which was of the greatest importance to the house of Fanad. In which case, he has preserved a reference which can be securely assigned to a date between the accession of Turlough of the Wine as the O'Donnell around 1380 and the death of Turlough Caoch MacSweeney entered in the annals in 1399, and most probably to the 1380s.

Interesting as is the value attached to the spear, it is his axe which clearly takes precedence among the galloglach's weaponry. Indeed by the second half of the fifteenth century it had evidently acquired an apparently ceremonial significance, when the annalists make particular reference to Enri MacCabe's burial at Cavan in 1460 having been 'attended by two hundred and eighty galloglas, armed with battle-axes'. The entry in the *Annals of the Four Masters* at 1495 mentions the O'Donnell's 'great little army' having included twelve score axemen (*tuagh fir*) to make a standing fight. An entry in the same annals seventeen years later specifies 'fifteen hundred axemen in Tyrconnell, Fermanagh and the province of Connacht' hired by the O'Donnell (presumably to augment his MacSweeneys) in preparation for war against the MacWilliam Burke. Both of those references can be taken to indicate the axe as the weapon which defined the galloglach as a fighting-man by the eve of the sixteenth century, and the same is confirmed by all the subsequent evidence from English observers.

Some modern historians, however, have expressed quite reasonable doubts as to when – or even whether – the long-staved axe was found in the hands of every galloglach.

After all, only one of the eight galloglas portrayed in the late fifteenth-century carvings at Roscommon carries an axe, while all the others shown are armed only with swords.

There can be no doubt that the warrior whose weapon was the long-handled axe would have required exceptional physical strength as well as masterly skill in its handling, but that need not detract from my own view that such a weapon would have been borne into battle by every galloglach, and probably from as early as the end of the fourteenth century when it can already be recognised as the characteristic weapon – if not yet the hallmark – of an élite professional warrior class. The physical qualities of the galloglas often seem to have been the first thing noticed about them in the Elizabethan accounts. Stanyhurst, for example, writes of them as 'men of great stature, of more than ordinary strength of limb', and Dymmok actually begins his description with the phrase 'picked and selected men of great and mighty bodies'. 'Picked and selected' does carry the clear implication of physique as the key qualification for recruitment, and so it would have been when it was the first requirement for handling the most prominent tool of the trade.

The axe – or, perhaps, more properly the *sparr* – was not his only weapon, of course, because a galloglach evidently also carried side-arms, certainly a sword in battle and, at the very least, a long-bladed knife bearing some resemblance to the later Highlander's dirk. He evidently also used heavier weapons other than the axe – a spear, perhaps a bow, or two-handed sword – and these would have been carried on to the field by his harness-bearer who stood ready to hand them to him as needed. Un-doubtedly there would have been some who took especial pride in their skill as axemen, just as others might have made a speciality of the two-handed sword, but every galloglach would have been trained to fight with the full range of his weaponry, among which the *sparr* clearly took precedence. In fact, so close was this association between warrior and weapon that not only was the fighting unit identified with the *sparr*, but on at least one occasion in the English state papers these axes themselves are casually referred to as 'galliglasses'.[21]

Whatever type – or types – of axe might have been in use by the warriors called 'galloglas' in the thirteenth century, the sixteenth-century evidence is quite clear as to the galloglach axe used as a cutting (as distinct from thrusting) weapon, and the Gaelic usage of the term *sparr* fully confirms all the documentary and graphic evidence for its standard fitting to a long handle. The same contemporary descriptions and illustrations of the design of its blade, however, vary widely. Sentleger's comparison with the 'axe of the Tower' can be taken to indicate something resembling the weapon still in ceremonial use by Yeoman Warders at the Tower of London, but scarcely corresponds to its description by Dymmok as 'somewhat like a shoemaker's knife', which suggests a closer similarity to the long-bladed Jedburgh stave well known in the Scottish Borders in the sixteenth century. The design of blade fitted to the pole handle of the galloglas weapon clearly cannot have been uniform, quite possibly varying between different parts of the country and depending upon how local smiths were able to meet the requirements of customers they supplied. In view of which, Professor Hayes-McCoy was quite surely correct in his conclusion that 'the galló-glach axe was so called, not because its blade approximated to any one type, but simply because it was an axe carried by the gallóglaigh'.[22]

There is another aspect to this galloglach axe with rather wider implication, however, and it lies in the practicality of handling a weapon which must have demanded not only physical strength but an exceptional level of skill, especially in the hands of warriors standing side by side in action, each of them wielding a lethal cutting-edge at the end of a pole up to two metres in length. The man engaging with an oncoming enemy – whether charging horse or galloglas similarly armed to himself – and concentrating on strenuous two-handed work with his own weapon would have been at risk of grievous injury from any miscalculation or incompetence on the part of a fellow-axeman fighting beside him. The ultimate strength of the galloglas in action, then, must have lain in their extraordinarily high standard of training in arms and discipline in action, and it was these which arguably made the greatest contribution to a quality of professional fighting-man formerly unknown among the Irish.

Unfortunately the documentary record of medieval Irish history does not include even a fragment of any galloglas training manual, so there is no real evidence of how, or at what age, a recruit acquired the expertise essential to the practice of his profession. It might, nonetheless, be reasonable to suggest at least some correspondence with what is known of the learned professions who had long represented a privileged class, even a part of the aristocracy, in Gaelic Ireland. The deepest roots of this custom of a learned professional class quite surely extended as far back into antiquity as the druidic culture of pre-Christian Ireland and, as was inevitable in a society anciently structured upon kinship, specialised learning and expertise, such as pertained to the lawyer (*brehon*) and the medic (*liagh*) for example, became the prerogative of particular families within which it was passed down the generations. Some such professional families, especially those of poets (*filidh*) and historian-genealogists (*seanchaidh*), attached themselves to noble houses with whom they assumed offices which became hereditary and endowed with landholdings, while others followed a more peripatetic lifestyle, moving around the country to find hospitality and reward from whoever might have need of their special skills.

At which point the parallel with the galloglas surely becomes immediately apparent. Just as there had been no warrior class in traditional Irish society, so there had been no comparable 'profession of arms'. The emergence of a warrior class can be seen as a consequence of the militarisation of Ireland which gathered momentum following the Anglo-Norman conquest, and with it the emergence of the galloglas as the military equivalent of the old learned professional class. The Hebridean and West Highland mercenary warriors had been organised on the basis of kin-group from the time of their first arrival in Ireland, so it was almost inevitable that their evolution into the *galloglaigh* would endow them with a status in Irish society similar to that of the *seanchaidh* and *filidh*. Whether or not they had acquired that social status by the end of the fourteenth century, two hundred years later they were almost casually included beside professional kindreds of the most ancient standing by an English law officer who concluded his summary of landholding in Fermanagh with a reference to 'lands given to certain septs privileged among the Irish, that is the lands of the chroniclers, rhymers and galloglas'.[23]

Another item of evidence of a similar vintage, and of useful bearing here, is found in the writing of Thomas Gainsford who described the form of education among Irish professional classes 'which live in a kindred, the father instructing the son or brother, and he his cousin or friend'.[24] Even though Gainsford was writing of the bards at that point, his following sentence refers to galloglas, and there can be little doubt of the mercenary warrior having learned his skills and discipline by much the same form of instruction, within a kin-group context and probably from youth, if not indeed from boyhood. The inevitably conservative character of such an educational process – by which the older generation taught the younger learning passed down to them through all the generations which had gone before – is widely recognised in what is known of the bards and the brehons, and may also explain why the galloglas of the sixteenth century appeared so similar to their warrior forebears of three or four hundred years earlier.

Even so, the greater part of a galloglach's professional education in the fifteenth and sixteenth centuries must have been concerned with the skills and tactics, codes and disciplines, mores and traditions which comprised an almost entire sub-culture built over generations of mercenary warrior experience in Ireland, and thus would have been at least unfamiliar if not quite unknown to those known as galloglas at the end of the thirteenth century. Indeed, while the galloglach could only have learned his trade within the context and culture of his professional kindred, much as the bard or brehon would have done, the authority of his learning was not so entirely dependent upon its antiquity and rigid preservation in the memory of countless generations. It hinged instead upon a system of tactics and techniques which could only have evolved in response to the changing – and unforgiving – demands of the military marketplace. So, too, the stoic code requiring galloglas to 'byde the brunt to the death' which was mentioned by some sixteenth-century English observers is more convincingly supported by the evidence of the annal record from the later fifteenth century onwards than in the earlier period, and so is best recognised as an aspect of the developing ethos of a military élite.

There is certainly good evidence of enduring feuds between galloglas kindreds – not so unlike an extreme form of professional rivalry – having becomed firmly embedded in their sub-culture. It is scarcely possible that these could have been imported from the Scottish homeland, and indeed they appear to have grown directly out of experience of mercenary warrior service in Ireland, of which, perhaps, the best documented example is the feud between the MacSweeneys and MacSheehys (the latter, of course, a kindred known only in Ireland, even though of originally Scottish Clan Donald descent).

In 1568, James Fitzmaurice of Desmond – who had assumed command while his kinsman the Earl was imprisoned in London – made a hosting into Kerry against Thomas Fitzmaurice or 'MacMaurice' as he is called by the Four Masters whose *Annals* preserve the most detailed account of events:

> The country was soon plundered, devastated, burned and totally ravaged by James and his forces. The greater part of [the people of] the country fled, carrying with them to Lixnaw as much of their cattle as they were able. James had so numerous an army that he pitched two very extensive camps on both sides of the town. He placed . . .

the Clann Sheehy with their battles and a proportionate number of the gentlemen and chiefs of the army at the eastern side of the town [of Lixnaw, seat of the Fitzmaurice knights of Kerry]; and he himself went, with that portion of the army which he wished to accompany him, to the west side of the town, so that MacMaurice and his people were in great jeopardy between them . . .

Eamonn MacSweeney was constable to MacMaurice at this time; and he had with him only a small party of galloglas of his followers, scarcely fifty men, the time of their service being expired. However, they did not think it honourable to depart from MacMaurice as this danger had overtaken him.

MacMaurice consulted with his constable who advised him to 'Resign thy luck and prosperity to fate and fortune this day and let us attack the Clann Sheehy, for against them our enmity and indignation are greatest.'

MacMaurice placed in order and array the small friendly forces that he had with him, and the Clann Sweeney were placed in the van to make the onset. No wealth or principality was, they thought, more agreeable to the Clann Sheehy and all those who were about them than to see them approach in this order, for they had rather subdue them [i.e. the MacSweeneys] on the spot (as they thought they could) than to remain awaiting them any longer.

MacMaurice and his people came up with the Clann Sheehy; and it was then that both parties made trial of the temper of their sharp spears, the strength of their battle-axes, the keenness of their swords, and the hardness of their helmets; and after having thus fought for some time, the fine forces of the Geraldines were worsted, and took flight and turned their backs from maintaining the field of battle. They were vehemently and swiftly pursued by the people of MacMaurice, who proceeded to wound and slaughter them; so that it would not be easy to reckon or enumerate all of the Geraldines and of the Clann Sheehy that fell in this defeat. There also fell Eamonn Og, son of Eamonn MacSheehy, chief constable to the Geraldines; also Murrough Balbh, son of Manus MacSheehy; Rory, son of Manus MacSheehy was taken prisoner; and many others besides these were slain or taken prisoner.

Interestingly, the obituary of Marcus MacSheehy, brother to the Eamonn Og killed at Lixnaw, is entered in the *Annals of the Four Masters* at the previous year when he was slain by the same Thomas Fitzmaurice of Kerry. Although the annalists do not say as much, there is every likelihood of the Kerry MacSweeneys' having been involved in the killing, which would have further fuelled the MacSweeney-MacSheehy feud. Its deeper roots, however, may well have extended further back in time to the great slaughter of the O'Neill's forces at Knockavoe in 1522, when 'Turlough MacSheehy with a great number of his people' was slain by MacSweeney galloglas with the O'Donnell. So great was the carnage at Knockavoe – some nine hundred warriors of the O'Neill alliance slain according to fully credible annal evidence – that it would have long burned in the memory and been passed between different branches of the same galloglas kindreds, so a clash of galloglas in Kerry was assuredly continuing a bloodfeud inherited from a battle in Donegal more than forty years before.

The Four Masters' account of Knockavoe is of unusual interest also by reason of its description of a galloglas engagement fought in darkness. The men – almost certainly MacDonnells – placed as sentinels around the camp saw the MacSweeneys advancing and rushed down to raise the alarm, reaching the encampment just as the attackers arrived:

> Coming into collision with one another they raised great shouts aloud . . . both forces were at striking and killing each other and mighty men were subdued, and heroes hacked, on either side men were hewed down. Scarcely did any one of them on either side know with whom he should engage in combat, for they could not discern one another's faces on account of the darkness of the night and their close entanglement with each other.

There is every reason to believe that a similar inter-tribal hostility had also grown up between the MacSweeneys and the MacDonnells, especially in the north where their respective employers since the thirteenth century had been the O'Donnells and O'Neills whose own rivalry extended so much further back into Ulster history. It was, in fact, in the year before the battle of Lixnaw that the O'Donnells (at the contrivance, it must be said, of English policy) inflicted the defeat at the ford of Farsetmore which at last brought down the proud Shane O'Neill. While the Four Masters' account indulges a measure of bardic licence – 'fierce and desperate were the grim and terrible looks that they cast at each other out of their starlike eyes' – the modern military historian Tim Newark's reconstruction of Farsetmore makes the convincing proposal that 'the galloglas of both sides, axes swinging, were engaged in a struggle fuelled not by the animosity of their pay-masters but by deeply inbred clan rivalry'.[25]

On the other hand, there were occasions when different branches of the same galloglas kindred found themselves facing each other in action, a situation in which residual clan loyalties were necessarily overruled by professional obligation. Such confrontations were more likely in the case of those kindreds who extended their employment most widely, and indeed virtually inevitable when an offshoot of the MacDonnells of Connacht moved eastward into Leinster and there found its way into government service. The most impressive example came about at Shrule on the border of Mayo and Galway in 1570, when Sir Edward Fitton, the new President of Connacht, moved in alliance with the Earl of Clanricard against the rebellious Burkes of Mayo. Professor Hayes-McCoy found the battle 'chiefly remarkable because of the representative forces of gallóglaigh engaged upon either side',[26] when the great strength of the Mayo Burkes lay in their MacDonnell galloglas of Connacht who were opposed by five battles of Clanricard's MacSweeneys, a battle of MacDowells, and the MacDonnells of Leinster under the command of Colla of Tynekille, 'Constable of Her Majesty's Galloglas'. While it was his name which headed the annalists' list of the slain, the outcome of Shrule cannot be considered truly decisive, because the Connacht onslaught, although fiercely resisted, did eventually break the government stand, of which only the Clanricard MacSweeneys held their ground. Flushed with triumph, the MacDonnells of Mayo pursued the flight of the broken ranks of their Leinster kinsmen, although unwisely in the event because the President and Earl remained overnight on the battlefield and so were able to claim formal victory for themselves on the following morning.

While conflict between septs of the same galloglas kindred in the service of contending employers can be considered 'characteristic of the mercenary service',[27] the same cannot really be said of internecine feuding within galloglas families themselves. There are numerous examples of assassinations and personal contests of arms between rival members of galloglas families, but conflict on a larger scale is entered in the *Annals of the Four Masters* as the 'battle of Ceann-salach' (probably Bloody Foreland on the Donegal coast facing Tory Island) 'fought by the Clann Sweeney of the Tuathas on the day of Samhain [1st November]' in 1554. Although the annalists do not say as much, the cause of contention would seem to have been a challenge to the chieftaincy of the Tuatha sept when the body count included the MacSweeney Tuath himself (Ewen Og, son of Ewen) with his brother Turlough Carragh on one side and their cousins Eamonn and Conor, sons of Donough, on the other, as well as 'numbers of other distinguished persons . . . slain on each side'. This was a battle between professional fighting-men, but not in their professional capacity and thus more typical of Irish nobility than of mercenary service, which would well correspond to the aristocratic style assumed for the kindred throughout the history preserved in their *Book of the MacSweeneys.*

There is no way of knowing whether other galloglas kindreds saw themselves in a similarly aristocratic mould or whether they were content with the social status of a professional class, but there must be some significance in the official record of Richard II's audience at Dundalk in 1395 which indicates his accepting the submission of the MacCabe of Clogher with just the same ceremony as he accepted that of the MacMahon of Oriel. By the last years of the fourteenth century, then, a constable of galloglas could be presented to a king of England and recognised as an Irish chieftain, while barely a hundred years earlier warriors called 'galloglas' appeared most to resemble the *amuis* or 'hirelings' and were principally remarkable for their Gaelic-Norse background and origin. So, too, it was their very similar character which prompted the annalists to recognise the West Highland contingents accompanying Robert the Bruce to Ireland in 1317 as 'many galloglas'. All of which would seem to point quite clearly to the middle decades of the fourteenth century as the crucial passage in the evolution of the galloglas phenomenon in Ireland.

There can be scarcely any doubt of the stimulus supplied to that evolution by the Bruce invasion, first of all in its demonstration that Anglo-Norman armies could be defeated by Scottish fighting-men and, almost certainly also, by the Hebridean and West Highland warriors who stayed on in Ireland to join others of their kin-group already resident and help supply the demand for mercenary forces. While it really cannot be claimed that the Bruce intervention marked the beginning of the Irish Gaelic resurgence, it must have provided fresh inspiration, if only in the damage done to Anglo-Norman hegemony in the north and military credibility elsewhere. A Gaelic-speaking Scottish warlord – in the person of Edward Bruce – had been able to claim kingship of Ireland and make a plausible attempt at an inaugural royal tour of the country, but of ultimately greater importance was the practical introduction of the Irish lords to the potential of a mercenary warrior type preferable to any they had previously employed.

For reasons already explained here, Irish warfare had already become heavily dependent upon mercenaries by the beginning of the fourteenth century. The inadequacies of the traditional muster comprising sub-chieftains and their followers had led to the employment of native Irish mercenaries in the form of kern, who would have been a poor match for Norman men-at-arms, particularly in open battle, even had they not presented their own problems in terms of discipline and reliability. It would have been for just those reasons that Irish chieftains took men-at-arms of Norman-Welsh origin into their own service because such warriors, known to the annalists as *sersenaigh* (the Irish form of the originally Old French term *serjeant* or 'common soldier') were organised into mercenary bands not unlike the *routiers* who became notorious in France during the Hundred Years' War. Such mercenary companies were known in Ireland by the strikingly similar name of *rúta* and may even, in some measure, have inspired or influenced the emergence of kern, because they evidently formed a component of thirteenth-century Anglo-Norman forces, and not least in Ulster where the de Burgh earls apparently had the MacQuillins as their hereditary constables (hence, of course, the 'Rout of the Mac-Quillins' mentioned earlier).

These *sersenaigh* are found also in Connacht, where the annal record indicates them as foot-soldiers, possibly as archers, serving under commanders with Norman and Welsh names, and where they were also employed by Irish magnates, although their loyalty in such service must often have been in doubt. As Dr Simms has suggested, their cultural background and its political associations would have placed such mercenary forces under natural suspicion of treachery. They might even have been more dangerously unreliable than the disreputable Irish kern when they could betray their Irish employers to Norman colonists, and so 'preferable from almost any point of view were the Scottish *gallóglaigh*'.[28]

Warriors from the Hebrides and West Highlands had ancient cultural links with the north of Ireland and, of course, spoke a closely similar form of the Gaelic tongue, yet their infusion of Norse blood and culture, with its traditionally warlike character, would have served to enhance their appeal as mercenary fighting-men. While such warriors had been resident in Ireland since the mid-thirteenth century, it would seem that their real military potential emerged only in the afterglow of the Bruce invasion, and with it the realisation that there were more – indeed, very many more – willing to join their kinsmen in Ireland. Their arrival and organisation as kin-groups under the command of their own nobility meant that they would not be prone to the problems of discipline which seem always to have dogged the kern. Neither – and unlike any native Irish soldiery – would they be distracted by local loyalties and obligations at so great a distance from their homelands and when their first loyalty was the professional obligation to their paymaster.

In strictly military terms, they were mail-armoured heavy infantry at least the equal of Norman men-at-arms. Perhaps more impressively, a galloglach wielding a long-handled axe could bring down a mounted knight, especially when the smaller native Irish steed – known as the *hobby* – supplanted the expensively imported heavy horses formerly ridden by the Anglo-Norman cavalry. On a cattle-raid, a company of galloglas were ideally equipped to form a defensive rearguard, which had been long considered by the Irish the more dangerous place on an expedition and the one in which it was the more noble for a warrior to fall. So too in open battle, a phalanx of axemen supplied a defensive stand – almost literally a 'castle of bones' – from behind which the traditional Irish horse could ride out to attack and to which they could return for shelter. Against a 'castle of stones', so long the great symbol of Norman conquest, the galloglas were a no less potent weapon when they were able to take such a fortress by heavily armed onset and afterwards to provide a garrison force when the stronghold was captured and occupied, as they were also able to do when the Irish began to build stone castles of their own.

It becomes quite clear, then, how immense must have been the contribution made by galloglas to the military potential of the native lords of Ireland and also, by extension, to their political resurgence through the fourteenth century. What it does not fully explain, though, is how the galloglas system came to be adopted also by the Anglo-Irish lords and eventually also by the government as it was extended into every province of Ireland and, by the fifteenth century, even within the Pale. It is often lamented – and with justice – that the annal record supplies the least indication of how the galloglas spread so extensively, but there is one key factor which suggests itself as the mainspring of that expansion.

That factor is perhaps most concisely identified in the phrase used by Sir John Perrot when he was faced with the Desmond rebellion in the early 1570s and insisted that he 'must have galloglas against galloglas'.[29] In fact, the President of Munster appointed by London in 1571 was really only expressing what had been known to every man of power in Ireland at least two hundred years before him: that the only form of soldiery effective against these heavy infantry was more of their own kind. There can have been very few, if any, greater or lesser lords in fourteenth-century Ireland who did not feel themselves surrounded by rivals or by rebels, and if one had galloglas then each of his potential opponents would have urgent need of them also. Thus must have been created the surging demand which led to the expansion of the galloglas system, first out of Ulster throughout Connacht and thenceforward across all Ireland, beyond the Gaelic Irish orbit and into that of the gaelicised Anglo-Irish lordships.

Perhaps the Burkes of Connacht might be offered as a helpful illustration at this point. In the spring of 1316 when the Bruce invasion was well under way, a mighty war-host which had been mustered out of Connacht to come to its support was blocked at Athenry by an Anglo-Norman force under Sir William Liath de Burgh, cousin to the Red Earl of Ulster, who inflicted upon it one of the bloodiest defeats ever suffered on an Irish battlefield and deprived Edward Bruce of potentially decisive reinforcement. It could also be said that it was this victory at Athenry which fully established the pre-eminence of his house in Connacht, and yet within less than twenty years the de Burgh earldom of Ulster had been extinguished and the line of William (hence the MacWilliam Burkes) in the west had renounced allegiance to the Crown. Nor was that renunciation in 1333 purely political, because they had also abandoned the Norman principle of succession by primogeniture in favour of the Gaelic Irish custom of tanistry and adopted Irish brehon law, so thoroughly had they become gaelicised in language and culture even as they approached the mid-point of the fourteenth century. All of which – as Professor Hayes-McCoy recognised – 'was typical of what went on all over Ireland in the aftermath of the Scottish invasion',[30] and if the Burkes had not at that time already begun to employ galloglas they were very soon to do so.

Their kinsmen of the Clanricard in Galway must have long had their galloglas by 1420 when a daughter of their house was taken to wife by an earl of Desmond 'and with her the galloglas of the MacSheehys first into Munster out of Connacht'.[31] There might even be reason to recognise that adoption of galloglas in place of the *sersenaigh* men-at-arms as the military index of gaelicisation among the Anglo-Irish, especially in view of the antipathy aroused by the blatantly Gaelic character and appearance of such warriors when they were introduced into the Pale in the fifteenth century.

While that suggestion perhaps applies in some cases, it does not generally hold good because the employment of galloglas was undertaken for military reasons rather than cultural preference. Yet undertaken it certainly was, even in the determinedly loyalist Butler lordship of Ormond (now the counties Tipperary and Kilkenny) by the 1430s, although perhaps with more caution than enthusiasm on the evidence of a ruling of that time which firmly restricted the billeting of galloglas to those in the personal retinue of the earl. For all the objections to galloglas as creatures of the 'wild Irish' and 'degenerate English' (the latter, of course, meaning the thoroughly gaelicised Anglo-Irish), the official objection to their presence in and around the Pale hinged upon their support by the system known as 'coyne and livery'. While this was essentially only an extension of the older custom of *buannacht* (or 'bonaght' in its anglicised form) by which a lord's mercenary fighting-men were supported by the civilian population of his territory, it was to become fiercely oppressive in the hands of the Anglo-Irish lords and yet also a central mechanism of the galloglas system.

The inevitable burden imposed by the retention of mercenary forces was the need for their remuneration – or other form of support – in respect of sword-service rendered. Where the employment was essentially casual, and especially when raiding and plunder were involved, mercenary assistance would have been most conveniently rewarded out of the proceeds of the enterprise. Indeed, an entry in the *Annals of the Four Masters* at 1564 tells of the O'Briens of Thomond (now County Clare) making war on the neighbouring MacNamaras, but being driven off after they had burned the town of Rossaroe:

> They [the O'Briens] afterwards brought from beyond the Shannon numerous mercenaries of the Clann Sweeney and Clann Sheehy and they had the ranging of the country and its preys and property in their power, until the expiry of their bonaght [i.e. period of employment]. There remained not, however, of cattle with the inhabitants of the country, the value of what was taken out of it by those soldiers for their services. [Or, put more simply, the O'Briens paid off their galloglas with more cattle than were left for the local people after they had gone.]

Plunder would almost always have supplied some component of the reward for mercenary service, even to the extent indicated by an entry in the same annals at 1571 and its vivid account of James Fitzmaurice's taking of

Kilmallock during the first Desmond rebellion. He had earlier occupied the town which held a strategically important position as the 'sally port of the Geraldines', but had been driven out by the English, and his attempt to regain possession was thrown back after taking heavy casualties. The Lord Deputy Sir Henry Sidney is said to have been so impressed by the heaps of slain galloglas that he knighted the garrison commander on the spot, but Sidney had not long returned to London before Fitzmaurice was to be back again, and his galloglas with him:

> Before sunrise in the morning, those who had gone to sleep happily and comfortably were aroused from their slumber by the furious attack made by the warlike troops of the Clann Sweeney and Clann Sheehy . . . and they proceeded to divide among themselves the town's gold, silver, various riches and valuable jewels, which the father would have acknowledged to his heir, or the mother to her daughter, on the day before. They were engaged for the space of three days and nights in carrying away the several kinds of riches and precious goods, its cups and ornamented goblets upon their horses and steeds to the woods and forests of Aherlow [south of Tipperary town]; and sending others privately to their friends and companions. They then set fire to the town and raised a black, thick and gloomy shroud of smoke about it, after they had torn down and demolished its houses of stone and wood; so that Kilmallock became the sanctuary and abode of wolves.

In better ordered times, of course, the support of permanently retained galloglas required a more formal arrangement of remuneration. As in the case of the MacSweeneys with the O'Donnell and wherever the office of constable became hereditary in branches of a kindred, the chief family appear to have been granted lands by their lord, thus endowing them with a semblance of aristocracy in their own right, even though it is not unlikely that such endowment may have originated as a substitute payment when other forms of funding were in short supply. Some similar grant to the MacSheehys of the Desmond galloglas provided them with land on which to live and to graze the livestock they had acquired either as legitimate payment or as their share of cattle-raiding.

The more widespread support of galloglas, particularly those employed under a casual or short-term arrangement, was by means of their being quartered upon the lord's tenantry. Some such system may even have been in operation by the last decade of the thirteenth century on the evidence of a traditional history of the O'Neills,[32] in which is made the claim that Donal O'Neill was the first to impose that obligation upon his people. That history was set down in the later sixteenth century and so represents a source of less than impeccable authority, but there is an item of closely contemporary evidence in its support. In 1297 the Archbishop of Armagh petitioned the same Donal of Tyrone – and the MacMahon of Oriel and Maguire of Fermanagh with him – to restrain their 'Scots and satellites' (i.e. galloglas and kern) from trespassing against his estates and tenantry, which infers that not only did the O'Neill have galloglas in his service but that some were also being supported, presumably on his behalf, by his sub-chieftains in Oriel and Fermanagh.

It would seem, then, that some system of bonaght was being used to maintain galloglas – at least by the O'Neill, and perhaps in emulation of the de Burgh earldom's 'bonaght of Ulster' – within seven years of the first reference to such warriors by that name in the annal record, and variant forms of the same system were to continue in use through the three centuries following. Rather more detail is indicated by the terms of Turlough Caoch MacSweeney's arrangement with the O'Donnell which allowed 'six scores of axes of *buannacht bona* [i.e. of axemen to be maintained] out of Tyrconnell itself'.[33] Even by the date of that agreement – probably in the 1380s, but certainly before 1400 – galloglas were already finding their way into the service of Anglo-Irish magnates of Connacht who similarly supported them by *buannacht*, but which was later to become 'coyne and livery'.

The term 'coyne' (sometimes *coign* or *coigny*) derived from the Irish *coinmeadh* or 'guesting', which would suggest the origin of the custom having lain in the old practice of a tribal king spending some part of his year on a circuit of his kingdom accompanied by his retinue and with them enjoying the full and forced hospitality of his chieftains (while the associated English term 'livery' adds accommodation of their horses to the arrangement). Galloglas would assuredly have formed part of such a retinue, probably from their earliest appearance in Ireland and certainly by the time of the O'Donnell's agreement with the MacSweeneys which endowed Turlough Caoch of Fanad with 'a gift in perpetuity [of] the making of a circuit of Tyrconnell once in a year, the spending of three nights in each house in Tyrconnell'. So too in the next generation, when Turlough's son and successor, Turlough Ruadh, is said by the *Book of the*

MacSweeneys to have accompanied the O'Donnell on his circuit of *Leath Chuinn* (or 'Conn's Half', meaning the north of Ireland).

Therein lies indication of the potentially oppressive character of 'coyne and livery'. While 'bonaght' would seem to have been sometimes imposed as a form of taxation – payable to the lord or to his constable and either in coin or in kind when it was estimated in terms of meat, cereal, butter or other commodity – coyne and livery was imposed by direct billeting. Galloglas and their attendants were thus quartered upon their employer's tenants or subjects who had to supply not only their food, drink and housing, but frequently their wages too, as is quite bluntly described in an official report of 1572:

> There will come a kern or a galloglach to lie in a churl's house; while he is there he will be master of the house; he will not only have meat, but money also allowed him, and at his departure, the best thing he shall see in the churl's house, be it a linen cloth, a shirt, mantle or such like. Thus is the churl eaten up.[34]

While there must have been wide variation in its form of imposition, the scope for abuse and corruption was virtually unlimited when it ranged from sheer brutality backed up by the lord's authorisation to merciful exemption from the obligation by means of payment of a bribe – called a 'foye' – to the constable. It is indeed almost impossible to imagine house-guests more unappealing to any medieval Irish host than a galloglas sparr with all their battle-gear, and bitter recollections of coyne and livery must have made their own contribution to the horror stories of 'slaught'ring gallowglass' which persisted in Irish folk culture long after the grim fighting-men themselves had passed into history.

If the oppressive coyne and livery can be blamed on the Anglo-Irish, then it would seem likely that their influence, no less than that of the native Irish lords, must be reflected in other aspects of the galloglas phenomenon as described in the sixteenth-century accounts. It was in Munster and in Leinster that Rich, Sentleger and Spenser, for example, encountered the galloglas they described, and yet these were the last of the Irish provinces to adopt the galloglas system.

Branches of the Hebridean and West Highland warrior kindreds first introduced into Ulster with the O'Donnells and O'Neills and into Connacht with the O'Connors in the thirteenth century found their way into the service of the Burkes of Mayo and Galway before the end of the fourteenth century, by which time they had become fully recognised for their military potential. It was not until the century following, though, that they became established in the Fitzgerald earldoms of Desmond in Munster and of Kildare in Leinster, and by that time their organisation must already have been shaped by service with Anglo-Irish paymasters. Thus it may very well have been that a great part of what was noticed about the galloglas by the sixteenth-century English observers – whether they realised it or not – owed more to the influence of the 'degenerate English' than to that of the 'wild Irish'. An illustrative example, although of passing interest rather than any great significance, occurs in Barnaby Rich's eye-witness account of the Desmond galloglas onslaught at Monasternenagh where he anglicises the ominous '*ooboo ooboo*' of the MacSheehys' battle-shout into 'hubbub', thus coining a word afterwards adopted into the English language. It would seem, though, that what he actually heard through the tumult of the action could only have been their version of the Fitzgerald war-cry '*Crom abu!*'.

At the same time as the organisation and maintenance of galloglas were changing as a result of employment by the Anglo-Irish magnates, so their tactics and techniques were being refined and adapted in response to the changing character of their battle experience. Certainly by the beginning of the fifteenth century they were being deployed in greater numbers by a wider range of paymasters who needed to field 'galloglas against galloglas', and as the century progressed they were fighting most often as heavy infantry units in open battle against warriors of their own kind. History knows of few, if any, places of education as unforgiving as the battlefield, so there can be little doubt of experience in the field having been swiftly absorbed into the training of novice galloglas throughout the fifteenth century to create the military élite described in the sixteenth-century accounts.

The galloglas phenomenon can thus be considered fully formed by the 1500s and, indeed, to have achieved the high peak of its history in 1504, because it was in August of that year that they bore the heat and burden of the day in what Professor Hayes-McCoy has justly recognised as 'the greatest battle fought by these professional axemen'.[35]

Knockdoe is described in one modern reference work of great authority as 'the largest ever battle fought between Irishmen'[36] and so, while the role of galloglas in the action is of principal importance here, an outline of the background might help to set it in context. The roots of the conflict were entangled in fifty years of feuding and personal hostility, but its immediate cause sprang from the war waged by Ulick Burke of Clanricard against the neighbouring O'Kellys who had long been allied to the rival Burkes of Mayo. Ulick's destruction of three O'Kelly castles and subsequent seizure of Galway town was in blatant contravention of a ten-year-old parliamentary edict which prohibited Irish and Anglo-Irish lords alike from making war without licence from the king's representative, so the O'Kelly appealed to the Earl of Kildare to take the punitive action required of him as Lord Deputy.

At which point the Great Earl takes up his crucial part in the story, because the range of forces he mustered to redress the O'Kelly's grievance bears impressive testimony to his stature as the most powerful man in the Ireland of his day. As Lord Deputy, Gerald Fitzgerald could call on his own relatively modest forces and those of the lords of the Pale, but his standing in the estimation of wider Ireland – reflected in his Gaelic name *Gearóid Mór* – enabled him to call also upon the Irish magnates of the north to join the unprecedented assembly of military might assessed by the *Annals of the Four Masters* as 'the forces of almost all *Leath Chuinn*'.

'For service such as this, at an unwonted distance from their homes, it is almost certain' – in the expert opinion of Professor Hayes-McCoy – 'that their warriors were mostly galloglas.'[37] So the O'Donnell would have brought his MacSweeneys, and the O'Neill tanist, who came in place of his father, would have had with him MacDonnells of Tyrone. The Great Earl, of course, had galloglas in his own service, estimated to be at least a hundred and twenty by the 1500s, and most of them assuredly MacDonnells of Leinster, but he had also eight score maintained for him by the MacMahon of Oriel. These would almost certainly have been MacCabes, as would those brought by the O'Reilly of Breifne, while the MacWilliam Burke of Mayo would have had his MacSweeneys and the O'Connor Roe his Connacht MacDonnells when their forces met up with those of the Great Earl as they entered Clanricard.

The only reliably detailed and reasonably contemporary description of the battle is that found in the chronicle of the St Lawrence family of Howth near Dublin,[38] one of whom had himself held a prominent command in the forces of the Pale at Knockdoe. While this *Book of Howth* account is written from a Palesman's viewpoint and sometimes promotes the interest of the participant family member at the cost of historical accuracy, there is no reason to distrust its evidence for the Earl's arrangement of his forces. He had evidently entered Clanricard's country before the enemy was ready to meet him and chose to take up his position around Knockdoe (anglicised from *Cnoc Tuagh*, appropriately 'the little hill of the axes') near Claregalway some few miles north-west of Galway town. The St Lawrence chronicler tells of the enemy seen approaching in the far distance while the Earl held his council of war, but by the evening 'the ground was appointed' for the action to come on the morrow:

> The bowmen [he] put into two wings [on either flank of] the billmen in the main battle of which the Lord of Howth was leader; the galloglas and the Irish in another quarter [presumably to the right of the main battle]; the horsemen on the left side . . . by reason there was a little wall of two foot height at the other side of the battle which would have troubled the horsemen. After all things [were] put in order they went to supper and after to their lodging to rest the residue of the night.

The chronicler's account of the council of war has the Lord of Howth insisting that 'I will be the beginner of this dance and my kinsmen and friends, for we will not hazard our English good upon the Irish blade', but that intention is contradicted not only by other evidence for the conflict, but most firmly by the Earl's own plan of action announced to his assembled commanders:

> Said the Earl, "Call to me the Captain of Galloglas, for he and his shall begin this game for it is less force of their lusties than it is of our young men." "I am glad," said the Captain, "you can do me no more honour by God's blood", and took the axe in his hand and began to flourish.

Athough the *Book of Howth* does not admit as much, its account leaves little doubt of the Earl's own galloglas having been ranged – just as he proposed – in the front rank of his main battle. 'It is less force of their lusties than . . . of our young men' must be taken to mean that his axemen were better able to contend with the Clanricard galloglas than were the infantry of the Pale. Ulick Burke would have with him the full strength of two MacSweeney septs – his own and those of his principal ally, the O'Brien of Thomond – in addition to whatever galloglas contingents had been brought to his muster by his other allies, notably the O'Carroll of Ely and O'Kennedy of Ormond.

The Lord of Howth is said by the chronicler to have urged his fellow-commanders to set their 'battles in perfect order this night, that every man shall know tomorrow his charge', so the Earl's forces would have been already in position looking out towards Lough Corrib and the distant hills of Connemara as the dawn broke and the enemy came into view on that morning of 19th August 1504. The most realistic modern estimates set the total numbers involved at around ten thousand troops, and three-fifths of those with the Earl, so the Clanricard forces would have been some four thousand strong.

Whatever the truth of the Howth chronicler's claim that the enemy had 'passed the night over . . . wagering, drinking and playing at cards, who should have this prisoner and that prisoner', there is no reason to doubt his description of the formation of Clanricard's advance on Knockdoe:

> And at morrow they prepared to battle in such order as their custom was; they set forward their galloglas and footmen in one main battle, and all their horsemen on their left side, and so came on . . .

The chronicle continues with an account of the Great Earl's address to his forces being interrupted 'by three great cries that disturbed his oration'. 'Do they think that we are crows that we will flee with crying?' was the Earl's response to what must have been the battle-shouts of MacSweeney galloglas in the van of the attack:

> With that the Irish galloglas came on, to whom the English archers sent them such a shower of arrows that their weapons and their hands were put fast together. MacSweeney, Captain of the Irish galloglas, came foremost and asked where was Great Darcy [a famously huge champion of the Pale]. Darcy answered that he was at hand which he should well understand. With that MacSweeney struck Darcy such a blow upon the helmet that he put Darcy upon his knees. With that Nangell, Baron of the Navan [another noble of the Pale], being a lusty gentleman that day, gave MacSweeney such payment that he was satisfied ever after. They fought terrible and bold.

It is unclear whether that last sentence applies to the individual combat or to galloglas of both sides already engaged around it, but the Howth chronicle tells no more of the ensuing action other than a peremptory concluding sentence: 'Awhile the Irish fled.'

There would seem to me to be just one likely reason for a Palesman failing to provide any further detail of a battle in which his side claimed a famous victory and that lies in the likelihood that the nobles and forces of the Pale played only the least part in the action. In view of Knockdoe having been predominantly a foot fight and of galloglas forming the greater part of both armies, there is scarcely any doubt of their having borne almost all of the brunt, and in very many cases, having done so 'to the death'. Writing more than a hundred years after the event, the Irish historian Sir James Ware – a contemporary of the Four Masters and, like them, with access to source material lost to more recent scholars – states that 'the fight was sharply continued for some hours with equal loss on both sides, but at last the victory fell on Kildare's side'.[39]

While the narrative of the action preserved in the annals is little better than a farrago of clichés, the entry in the *Annals of Ulster* of the death-toll suffered by the Clanricard alliance is so much more plausible than the 'reported nine thousand' claimed by the *Book of Howth* that it might well have some genuine authority:

> Howbeit, the battle is gained on the MacWilliam [of Clanricard] and on the O'Briens and slaughter is inflicted upon them. And the place wherein were nine battles of galloglas in compact array there escaped not alive of them but one thin battle alone.

Sir James Ware's account corroborates the Ulster annalist's figures with the confident statement that 'on Ulick Burke's side there fell about two thousand men'. At a strength of eighty sparrs to a battle and each sparr made up of a galloglach with one or two armed attendants, the loss of eight full battles and part of a ninth would well enough approximate to Ware's body-count of two thousand. It is still possible, of course, that both accounts exaggerate the Clanricard losses, but there can be no question of their having been extraordinarily heavy.

As to the losses suffered by the victors at Knockdoe, the same entry in the *Annals of Ulster* adds that 'there fell many multitudes of the forces of the Earl on the other side', which bears interesting comparison with Sir James Ware's recollection of having seen a reference in the 'White Book of the Exchequer' (which was lost in the Dublin fire of 1610) to the effect that 'in the same bloody battle there was not one Englishman hurt'. The two claims need not necessarily be contradictory, when Ware's reference does specify *Englishmen* – by which he can only mean Palesmen – and the *Book of Howth* is no less specific as to the Earl's separation of 'the galloglas and the Irish' from the forces of the Pale. The unmistakable inference must be that it was the galloglas of both sides who did almost all of the hand-to-hand fighting at Knockdoe.

The Clanricard advance into an arrow storm – a situation in which heavy infantry were always at a disadvantage – must have taken its own toll of casualties. Engaging first with the Earl's galloglas standing in the front ranks of his main battle and very soon, if not immediately, afterwards coming under attack from superior numbers of galloglas moving in on their left flank, the Clanricard MacSweeneys would seem to have charged into a death trap. Yet this was exactly their kind of fighting, the close combat with edged weaponry every galloglach was trained and armed for, and the outcome at Knockdoe would seem never to have been a foregone conclusion. Indeed, the Earl himself is said by the Howth chronicler to have been visited on the midnight before the conflict by one of Clanricard's men he had known as a horseboy years before who urged him to flee for his life, saying 'it was but folly to fight'. The Great Earl, however, was a man familiar with the ways of the Irish, English and Anglo-Irish at war and well able to calculate the odds of the battle ahead when he had proposed to the constable of galloglas that 'he and his shall begin this game'.

After some hours of what must have been the most savage – and closely contested – 'hand stripe', what remained of the Clanricard galloglas were thrown back and pursued along the banks of the Clare river, where local tradition claims to know of the places where bands of survivors who turned to make a stand against the oncoming pursuit were at last cut down. For all the shortfall in quality and quantity of the evidence, there is still so much about this great fight around the 'hill of the axes' that offers vivid illustration of the galloglas phenomenon at the high point of its history. The single combat between rival champions, for example, is known from sources of history and tradition to have been a feature of Irish warfare at least as early as the seventh century. It was still in evidence through the Hiberno-Norse period, most especially in the *Cogadh* account of Clontarf, and so would have naturally fallen to the galloglas in their capacity as royal bodyguards soon after their first appearance in Ireland in the thirteenth century.

If there is a core of truth in the local Galway tradition of survivors having turned from retreat to face almost certain death in last stands along the banks of the Clare – and there is no reason at all why there should not be – then it bears full testimony to the stoicism of their warrior ethos. There is one passing reference in the *Book of Howth* account of Knockdoe, however, which is of ultimately great importance in the history of the galloglas. It occurs immediately after 'the Irish fled', when a horseman was caught up in the maelstrom of the retreat and 'a soldier out of Dublin struck him with a gun with both hands and so beat out his brains'. This is, in fact, the very first reference to a firearm – as distinct from an artillery piece – found in the historical record of warfare in Ireland, and there is no small irony in its occurrence in this greatest of all galloglas battles, because it was the hand-gun which was to play a great part in displacing the mail-armoured axe-man from his position of pre-eminence on the Irish battlefield.

The disappearance of the galloglas phenomenon from Irish warfare does seem now to have been remarkably sudden. They had been more prominent than ever before in the annal record of the first nine decades of the the sixteenth century – as they were also in the contemporary English accounts of the same period – because, of course, Ireland in the throes of the Tudor re-conquest was effectively a country at war. After the fall of the house of Kildare in 1537, government of Ireland could no longer be trusted to an Anglo-Irish aristocracy tainted by gaelicisation and so was passed by London into the hands of English-born administrators.

Their task was to obtain the submission of Irish and Anglo-Irish lords to the Crown, and they were swift to recognise the importance of galloglas to its accomplishment. For all the official disapproval of anything associated with Gaelic Ireland, a MacDonnell of Tynekille had been formally appointed Constable of Her Majesty's Galloglas in the decade before Sir John Perrot was demanding 'galloglas against galloglas' when faced with the first Desmond rebellion in Munster. Nor were they slow to identify the key role of mercenaries in the resistance to the government when they sought to obtain submission of galloglas chieftains and thereby deprive rebel lords of access to crucial military manpower. Sir Henry Sidney supplied his own frank account of using just such a stratagem against the MacWilliam Burke in 1576:

> Out of the county of Mayo, came to me to Galway seven principal men of the Clandonnells, all by profession mercenary soldiers by the name of galloglas. These humbly submitting themselves and their several lineages to her Majesty and binding themselves by indenture and hostage never to serve any but with the allowance of the Governor [of Connacht]. Truth it is, I was informed that MacWilliam Eughter would not come to me and therefore I drew this plot, that I won his chief force from him in getting these Clandonnells.[40]

By the mid-sixteenth century, though, a new type of mercenary warrior was being recruited by the native Irish lords from exactly the same source as had been the galloglas two or three hundred years earlier. These were the fighting-men called 'redshanks', or sometimes 'new Scots', who could be imported from the Hebrides and West Highlands on an almost industrial basis, as and when they were needed, employed by the season and afterwards returned to their Scottish homeland. There has been a tendency for some historians to confuse these redshanks with galloglas, even though the contemporary sources never do so. Both were of the same region of origin and, indeed, some redshanks were of the same original kin-group as some galloglas kindreds. So too, both were fighting-men of mercenary type, but there the similarity stops short. Galloglas kindreds had been permanently resident in Ireland – and raising new generations with Irish wives – for two hundred years by the time of the first arrival of redshanks and were considered to be Irish in their every aspect. Perhaps more importantly here, they were a military institution which had been almost entirely formed in Ireland and recognised there as an Irish professional class with a sub-culture all of its own. Neither their character nor their social status bore comparison with that of these 'new Scots', whose essential value lay in the numbers of hardy fighting-men they could supply to Irish paymasters facing a formidable new enemy in the form of a sixteenth-century regular army.

The introduction of redshanks in ever greater numbers by the rebel lords of the north through the middle decades of the sixteenth century does, in fact, point to their having already found the galloglas system wanting, when it was incapable of providing mercenary forces in the numbers needed to face the size of army Elizabeth's government could field. When rebel lords were crushed and their estates forfeit – as in Munster after the defeat of the last Desmond rising in the early 1580s – their galloglas were scattered afield, some in search of freelance employment in a declining market, others just drifting into banditry. While the better-appointed septs were considered 'gentlemen' by English administrators, and their members thus enabled to benefit from the policy of surrender and regrant in becoming landowning subjects of the Crown, the less fortunate were lost among the hungry tide of 'mere Irish' at large in a wasted land.

In the last analysis, though, it was the changing character of Irish warfare in the last decade of the sixteenth century which brought about the disappearance of the galloglas. Other than some surnames perhaps, virtually nothing of the galloglas who fought at Knockdoe is recognisable in those who served Hugh O'Neill, Earl of Tyrone, in the last stand of Gaelic Ireland against Elizabethan re-conquest. While there were some MacDonnells with O'Neill in 1595, in which year his forces triumphed at Clontibret, they were no longer the élite axe-men of earlier days because Irish battlefields had at last admitted the ascendancy of pike and shot.

Tyrone's initial military successes are generally and justly attributed to reforms he himself pioneered when he found the supply of redshanks strangled by Elizabeth's agents in Scotland and those galloglas who could be persuaded to retrain with new weaponry unavailable in the numbers needed. His response was to adopt and expand the native bonaght in the north of Ireland, recruiting by public proclamations made each spring for the campaigning season, offering a soldier's pay to any able-bodied man of whatever class, and employing Spanish officers and Irishmen who had fought in Spain and the Low Countries to train a militia able to fight an effective guerilla war with firearms. Their quality greatly impressed one English officer who complained that the Irish had 'drawn the greatest part of their kern to be musketeers, and their galloglas pikes, they want no furniture either of muskets, fowling pieces, calivers, swords, powder and shot'.[41]

In the end, of course, Tyrone's 'Nine Years' War' met with failure when a dawn attack on English forces was defeated at Kinsale in Cork on Christmas Eve in 1601. Any galloglas who fought on with him to the last – and of his own MacDonnells as well as of his ally Red Hugh O'Donnell's MacSweeneys some there must have been – would have been merely pikemen in support of kern now armed with arquebuses. So perhaps it is fitting to borrow a meagre epitaph from Thomas Gainsford who himself had fought against O'Neill's army at Kinsale:

'The name of galloglas is in a manner extinct'.[42]

IV

PERSPECTIVES AND PARALLELS

'Out of the northern airt it is that succour comes'

Writing in the mid-1160s, the anonymous author of the *Cogadh Gaedhel re Gallaibh* described the Scandinavian impact on Ireland in terms 'of hardship, and of injury, and of oppression' inflicted by 'sea-cast floods of *gaill* . . . valiant, wrathful, foreign, pagan people' out of the north. Yet barely some two hundred and fifty years later, when the Gaelic resurgence against Anglo-Norman dominion had come into its full flood, a bard addressing the O'Neill was able to declare that 'out of the northern airt it is that succour comes'.[1]

It was the galloglas, of course, to whom the bard's declaration referred, and therein lies some obvious irony when they were in great part descended – in blood and in culture – from the same 'valiant, wrathful, foreign, pagan people' denounced by the *Cogadh*. Relations between the Irish and the descendants of the Norse settled west-over-sea had been entirely and inevitably transformed through the five hundred years which separated the first viking raids from the first notice of galloglas by the annalists. The Scandinavian enclaves in Ireland itself – first feared as pirate fortresses and afterwards invariably distrusted, even whilst in submission to the sovereignty of Irish kings – seem to have retained their own distinctly separate character until, one by one, they succumbed to the Norman conquerors.

The Norman conquest can be seen now as a point of most crucial significance in the development of a newly close relationship between the Gaelic lords of the north of Ireland and the Gaelic-Norse aristocracy of the Hebrides and West Highlands through the thirteenth century, and yet therein lies a further irony because the Normans were themselves a people descended from an originally Scandinavian settlement formally established on the Seine some three hundred and fifty years earlier. Their origins in northern France run closely parallel – although not precisely contemporaneous – with those of the *gall-gaedhil* of Argyll and the Isles, when both had begun as viking forward bases which drew in further waves of settlers whilst absorbing the culture and customs of the neighbouring natives.

The same parallel, however, does not long hold for the subsequent development of the two settlements. Normandy so swiftly adopted the language and institutions of the Franks that it was transformed from a Scandinavian colonial outpost into a feudal French province within little more than a generation and there is, for example, no evidence of the Norse tongue in use there after 940. It is thought, though, that some Norse loanwords bearing on matters maritime found their way into Norman French and thereafter into the modern language, as indeed was certainly also the case with Scottish Gaelic. Much like the Normans in northern France, the Norse settlement along Scotland's western seaboard adopted the dominant local tongue, although over a rather longer period of time by reason of the geographical extent of the territory and, at least in the north, the power and influence of the Orkney jarls enduring into the second decade of the eleventh century. While the *gall-gaedhil* were apparently Gaelic-speaking by the mid-ninth century when they are first noticed by that name in the Irish annals, more than two hundred years may have passed before the language – as the dominant tongue of the Norse kingdom of Man and the Isles – fully penetrated the northernmost extent of the *Innse-Gall*.

All of which is perhaps best illustrated when seen from an Irish perspective. The ancient links between the north of Ireland and the west of Scotland had been dramatically severed by the advent of the northmen who were recognised by the Irish – in the Isles and within Ireland itself – as 'foreigners', the term *gall* being applied so exclusively to them as to become a virtual synonym for 'Norse'. Indeed, it continued in that same usage into the thirteenth century when the *gall* component of galloglas served to indicate the Norse element in their background just as it had earlier identified the *gall-gaedhil* of Argyll and the Hebrides as creatures of a Celtic-Scandinavian cultural province. The application of the same term *gall* to the Anglo-Normans after their invasion of Ireland, by contrast, serves to identify them simply as 'foreigners'. The Norse character of their origin may have been known earlier to the Irish (especially in view of a reference in the *Cogadh* to a possibly Norman warrior among the northmen at the battle of Clontarf), but even if still remembered by the late 1160s it would have been scarcely recognisable in the Anglo-Norman invaders.

By that time also, the feudalisation of the Scottish realm under its Norman-influenced Canmore kings had already begun to affect the out-lands of the west. The invasion of the Clyde in 1164 by Somerled's last great fleet – which included, incidentally, a contingent of Dublin Norse – has been convincingly recognised by a modern authority on the period as 'a pre-emptive strike against the expanding Stewart lordship in the west of Scotland',[2] and can thus be seen as the response of the Gaelic-Norse to the threatening ambition of a Norman baron sponsored by the royal house of Canmore. The death of Somerled in the course of that failed enterprise certainly did not go unnoticed in Ireland where it was entered with some prominence by the annalists, one of whom afforded Somerled the full dignity of 'king of the Innse-Gall'.[3] Within less than a century, of course, not only had another Canmore king of Scots firmly demonstrated his ambitions of sovereignty over Argyll and the Hebrides, but the Gaelic lords of Ulster had faced a similar – if not, indeed, more urgently aggressive – threat when the armies of Ireland's Norman conquerors advanced northward into their territories.

There is every reason, then, to propose the common ground of similar experience having revived ancient links between the Gael of northern Ireland and of the west of Scotland into the newly close relationship which brought Duncan MacDougall to fight for the O'Donnell in 1247 and Dugall MacRuari to slay an Anglo-Norman sheriff on the Connemara coast eleven years later. So, too, when political alliance was customarily sealed by marriage, daughters of Somerled's line and of other West Highland kindreds are found as the brides of Irish chieftains through the second half of the thirteenth century – and with them to Ireland came the first of the warriors called galloglas.

The warlike trait invariably – and not at all unreasonably – associated with the viking does appear to have passed down to his Norman and Gaelic-Norse descendants, and yet developed along distinctly different lines in each of those two cultures. While the spirit which underlay the Scandinavian expansion can still be recognised in the thrust of Norman conquest southwards into Italy and Sicily, eastwards to Antioch and, of course, over the Channel to England, their viking warrior legacy would seem to have been promptly recast into the 'military' mould which the Germanic cultures, such as that of the Carolingian Franks, had inherited from the Roman Empire. Roman imperial influence had made scarcely any impact upon the Celtic outlands of the far west, and so at that extent of the Scandinavian expansion, where northman and native appear to have inherited their similar 'heroic' traditions from the warband cultures of the Dark Ages, the warrior trait of the viking was to retain rather more of its original character long into the medieval period.

Impressive illustration of this sector of Celtic-Scandinavian common ground is found in the historical record of the raising of fighting forces in Argyll and the Hebrides when it indicates much the same system having remained essentially unchanged through almost a thousand years. For obvious reasons, the sea had always been the natural thoroughfare of the Hebrides and the adjacent mainland, so warfare was predominantly naval in character and, when warships – whether oceangoing curraghs or West Highland galleys – were driven by sail and oar, the crew-member was also the warrior. A reference implying the importance of 'ship-service' in Scotic Dalriada is found in evidence bearing on the sixth century, but greater detail of obligation for Dalriadic military/naval service in the seventh century is preserved in the *Senchus fer nAlban*, a survey of taxation and military obligation which assesses local capacity in terms of 'houses' and consistently specifies 'two seven-benchers [i.e. twenty-eight crewmen] from every twenty houses for sea-campaign'.[4]

A closely comparable system of recruitment of warship crews was in operation in Scandinavia – on a national basis by the tenth century, although probably earlier as a local arrangement – where it was known as *leidang*, and, specifically in west Norway, divisional districts called *skipreida* were obliged to provide a vessel, its crew and supplies. Variations upon that same principle of ship-service are found throughout Scandinavian Scotland and continued through the medieval period, an essentially similar system supplying crews for the galleys of the Lords of the Isles as for the longships of the northmen and the curraghs of the Celtic Scots of Dalriada. Even so, this was a levy under obligation, effectively a system of conscription as distinct from one of professional military service, and yet there is clear evidence for fighting-men from Argyll and the Hebrides known as a distinct professional warrior type in the north of Ireland by the second half of the thirteenth century. Alastair Campbell of Airds has thrown some light on the question in his recent history of the Clan Campbell where he suggests that the 'professional warrior was long a feature of the social make-up of the clan, although little mention is made of him . . .'

> Leadership in war has a long history in this country of being a gentleman's profession; the professional warrior – Professor Allan MacInnes refers to them as *buannachen* – was billeted out among the clan and was not expected to labour for his keep. Surplus in rents would also contribute to the upkeep of a force of armed men in the

chief's service, and it may be that this occupation was filled by many
of the younger sons of the house who make such fleeting appearances.[5]

If the eminent Campbell historian is correct – and I am increasingly
persuaded that he must be – then he has pointed almost decisively to the
origin of the galloglas phenomenon, especially when his further suggestion
that 'their services could be offered, for instance, as a daughter's *tocher*' (or
dowry) bears such immediate correspondence to the annalists' notice of the
'eight score warriors' brought to Derry by Alan MacRuari accompanying
his niece to meet her O'Connor bridegroom in 1259.

The Scottish Wars of Independence must have served to introduce West
Highlanders to frontline military experience in greater numbers than ever
before and thus created along Scotland's western seaboard a potential
reservoir of battle-hardened and weapon-trained warriors to meet the surge
in demand stimulated in Ireland by Edward Bruce's invasion. Meanwhile,
the Bruce ascendancy in Scotland had played its own part in generating the
supply to meet that demand when its impact upon the power structure of
Argyll added to the numbers of displaced or dispossessed members of the
Gaelic aristocracy who saw a new opportunity for themselves – and for
fighting-men loyal to them – in the profession of arms across the North
Channel. It is tempting to wonder whether at least some of those who
chose to become galloglas in Ireland were more attracted by the Gaelic
resurgence there than they were by the Bruce achievement of Norman
conquest in Scotland, but much more certain is the attraction that their
own Gaelic-Norse background must have held for Irish magnates looking
to expand their mercenary forces.

There can, I think, be no doubt that the Hebridean and West Highland
fighting-men who emerged as Ireland's élite warrior class in the fourteenth
century were following in military footsteps left on the country by the
earlier phases of Scandinavian impact. The Irish recognition of Norse
superiority in warfare is fully attested by twelfth-century sources, where it is
clearly implied by Gerald of Wales and frankly admitted by the *Cogadh*,
and further confirmed by more recent archaeological findings which
indicate Irish attempts to imitate the war-axe and long-bladed sword
introduced by the northmen. That same superiority – most particularly
in body armour and weaponry – would have been recognised by the Irish in
the Hebridean and West Highland warriors who arrived in the thirteenth

century, thus endowing them and those who followed them as galloglas with the warlike superiority long associated with the Norse.

Nor does there seem to be any doubt, at least in current Irish historical thinking, as to the mercenary fighting-man having been a Scandinavian introduction into Ireland. Dr Simms points to the appearance of the term *suartleach* in Irish sources of the eleventh and twelfth centuries and to its apparent origin in the Norse word *svartleggja* ('mercenary soldier'). The *Cogadh*, for example, claims that the Norse, at the height of their power in Munster, billeted a *suartleach* on every house and conscripted the most able member of every family 'to take wages (*tuarastal*), the day on which he embarked on board ship with his lord . . . supplied with provisions as if he was at home'. However accurate the evidence of that source, the billeting of foreign mercenaries and conscription of the natives for paid fighting service had not been known earlier in Ireland and are thus most realistically recognised as Scandinavian introductions which were afterwards extensively imitated by Irish magnates.[6] Indeed, the Irish term *buanna* meaning a mercenary (from which, of course, *buannacht* for the custom of his billeting upon the populace) is believed by one authority to have been a loanword with its origin in the Norse term *bòandi* for 'a husbandman or tiller of the soil'.[7]

The prime example of a mercenary tradition in the Scandinavian homeland is that of Jomsvikings, a highly-disciplined community of professional warriors who fought for their living in the summer and wintered in their fortified garrison camp on the south Baltic coast. The most substantial account of their activities and organisation is found in the Icelandic *Jomsvikinga Saga* set down around 1200, semi-legendary in character and yet with a genuinely historical core which has been supported by archaeological investigation of three fortress sites in Denmark closely corresponding to the *Jómsborg* of the saga and assigned to the later tenth and eleventh centuries.

Although drawing on the same Scandinavian wellsprings, there are few striking similarities between the Jomsviking tradition and Norse-inspired mercenary soldiering in medieval Ireland. At the south-eastern extent of the Scandinavian expansion, however, a wide range of closely contemporary sources – Byzantine and Russian chronicles as well as the inevitable Icelandic sagas – tell of other professional fighting-men called by various forms of the name 'Varangians' who do represent a much closer parallel to the galloglas. There had been earlier raiding and trading from Scandinavia's eastern shores through the Gulf of Finland, but by the early ninth century Scandinavian venturers of Swedish origin and known as the *Rus* had evidently established settlements in the northern reaches of the country later named for them as Russia. The Scandinavian origins of Russia are almost as complex as they have long been controversial, but might be most simply summarised in terms of a Scandinavian warrior aristocracy settled first in the region around Novgorod, hunting the northern forests and imposing submission upon the native peoples before looking further to the south where their recognition of a splendoured centre of wealth and power is reflected in their name of *Mickligardr* for the Byzantine capital of Constantinople.

Their way to Byzantium lay along the great Russian rivers, and so Kiev on the Dnieper, which offered the assembly point for their fleets bound for the Black Sea and Constantinople, was seized from the Khazars to become the new capital centre of the Rus. They first descended on *Mickligardr* as raiders and with a savagery exceptional even by viking standards, but detailed Byzantine records of trading treaties show a more mutually beneficial relationship to have been established by the first decade of the tenth century. Hazardous rapids punctuating the lower course of the Dnieper made it necessary for traders and their cargoes to travel some sections of the route by portage, which then exposed them to attack by raiders of the Pechenegs, a fierce Turkish people of the region. Consequently, companies of fighting-men were formed to provide defensive escort for the trading fleets, and from these was to emerge the famous Varangian Guard of Byzantium. At the end of the tenth century – traditionally in 989, but possibly in the following year – Vladimir of Kiev reached a new understanding with the Byzantine emperor, under which the Rus adopted the Orthodox faith and Vladimir himself took the Emperor's sister as his wife with lands in the Crimea as her dowry. Vladimir's own gift to the bride's brother was a force of six thousand fighting-men who formed the original company of the Emperor's Varangian Guard, initially as his personal bodyguard and later as an élite warrior component of the Byzantine forces, fighting for the Empire – and as mercenaries, of course, for their pay – through more than two hundred years until their last heroic stand on the walls of Constantinople when the Empire fell at last to the Fourth Crusade in 1204.

Like the Hebridean Norse in Gaelic Scotland and around much the same time, the Rus were Scandinavian settlers of warlike character and viking origin who adopted the tongue of the dominant host community (in their case, the Slavonic which Vladimir demanded be used as the language of the litany when he accepted the Orthodox faith and thus created the Russian Orthodox church). So too the galloglas and the Varangians, both of them mercenaries and of ultimately Scandinavian origin; both came to represent an élite professional warrior type whose characteristic weapon was the war-axe and, however incidentally, both appear to have made their first entry into the historical record by way of association with marriage treaties.

There may be another interesting similarity too, because the name 'Varangian' became a synonym for 'Scandinavian' – just as did the term 'gall' in Ireland – and yet is thought to have had its origin in an oath of loyalty taken by mercenary warriors either to each other or, perhaps more probably, to the traders they were to escort whilst taking valuable cargoes through dangerous territory. 'Varangian' would thus have had the original meaning of 'oath-taker', and so it is curious to find Stanyhurst saying of the galloglas that each one, on recruitment, took a great oath (*magna religione jurat*) that under no circumstances would he turn his back on the enemy,[8] a claim which corresponds well enough to Dymmok's description – supported by Sentleger – of warriors 'that do not lightly abandon the field, but byde the brunt to the death'.

While it would be reasonable to assume that the first six thousand warriors gifted by Vladimir to the Emperor were Rus and of predominantly Swedish ancestry, there is plentiful evidence for later recruits to the Varangian Guard being drawn from the widest orbit of the Scandinavian world. By the eleventh century, Norse warriors who had come east as political exiles were finding their way from Russia into the mercenary service of the Byzantines, the most famous of them being Harald Sigurdsson who had fled Norway after the death of his brother King (later Saint) Olaf at the battle of Stiklestad in 1030. Harald had been brought to Russia by Rognvald Brusasson, the future jarl of Orkney, and afterwards made his way on to Constantinople where he distinguished himself in action with the Varangian Guard in Sicily, Italy and Bulgaria before entanglement with the scandal and intrigue of the Byzantine court forced his return to the north and to greater fame as the Norwegian king best remembered as Harald Hardradi.

Of particular bearing here is the description of his *Saga* by its modern editors as 'the story of a warrior's progress . . . essentially the life and career of a professional soldier starting with a battle – Stiklestad where Harald is wounded – and ending in battle, thirty-six years later at Stamford Bridge'.[9] Just a few weeks after that battle, another fought on the sands of Hastings was to eventually deliver a new influx of recruits to the Varangian Guard. The Norman conquest of England, and specifically the harrowing of Northumbria which came in its wake, resulted in some numbers of northern English (or effectively Anglo-Danish) warriors being driven into exile and re-appearing in the ranks of the Varangian Guard after 1170. References found in the sagas confirm Icelanders also having served with the Varangian Guard from the second quarter of the eleventh century onwards. Indeed, the historian H. R. Ellis Davidson has recognised in the saga evidence 'a general assumption that a visit to Byzantium was the expected thing of a brave man who wanted to win wealth . . . the later Viking Age equivalent to raiding in the Baltic in earlier times'.[10]

All of which bears testimony to a custom of mercenary warrior service having extended to the furthest reaches of the Scandinavian expansion, but might still seem very far removed from the western seaboard of Scotland. If so, it will be as well to mention that two of the Icelanders with the Varangian Guard in Byzantium were direct descendants of the Ketil Bjornsson who was claimed as the ancestor of a prominent Icelandic family and who was also noticed by the Irish annalists as the leader of a *gall-gaedhil* warband in 857, an entry of some significance because it represents one of the earliest appearances of the *gall-gaedhil* in the annal record.[11]

Like the Varangian Guard, who were a Byzantine institution although predominantly Scandinavian in origin, the galloglas were named for the Norse element in their Gaelic Scottish background and yet represented an exclusively Irish military phenomenon. There, however, that parallel ends because the Varangians did not become Byzantines in any sense even approximating to the way that the galloglas kindreds became undeniably Irish.

As far as I have been able to discover and for all the anachronism of his reference to them, Shakespeare was alone among Elizabethan writers in associating galloglas with 'the Western Isles' or, indeed, with any region of Scotland. In all the other sixteenth-century accounts, the only 'Scots' in Ireland (with the possible exception of the MacDonnells of Antrim) were the 'redshanks' imported to fight by the season and those who survived shipped home at its end. The galloglas they recognised as the most formidable fighting-men among the 'wild Irish' – and, in fact, they were substantially correct to do so.

There is no evidence for any further reinforcement of the galloglas kindreds from the Hebrides or West Highlands after 1400, and while the names of almost all galloglas constables on record are those of the six kindreds of Gaelic Scottish origin, the men under their command were of Irish birth and, probably also in many cases, of Irish descent. Indeed, hereditary constables whose families had been resident in Ireland since at least as early as the mid-fourteenth century were invariably the sons of Irish mothers, as had been their fathers, their grandfathers and still more generations in the male line. Just as intermarriage with the Gaelic Irish is recognised as the principal agency of gaelicisation of the Anglo-Irish, so likewise it would have brought about the eventual 'hibernicisation' of the galloglas kindreds.

There is every reason, then, to consider the galloglas as Irishmen by the end of the fifteenth century, and yet the sub-culture which distinguished them as Ireland's professional warrior class into the later sixteenth century preserved much that had been brought out of the *Innse-Gall* by their forebears three hundred years before. Nor can that legacy be understood merely in terms of mail shirts and war-axes, because in the stoicism and the savagery which marked out the galloglas on Irish battlefields there can be recognised the last unmistakable echo of the Scandinavian impact on the Celtic west.

AN AFTERWORD FROM THE ISLES

'And this Man was call'd Galloglach'

'The finest ensemble of medieval sculpture to survive anywhere in the Western Isles' – in the judgement of the most recent official survey of monuments in the region – decorates a tomb inside the sixteenth-century St Clement's church at Rodel on the southern tip of Harris.[1] Dean Donald Monro's account of his travels through the Isles in 1549 credits the building of the church at Rodel to 'MacLeod of Harris', by whom was meant the Alexander MacLeod of Harris and Dunvegan who had died just a few years earlier. It was he who also commissioned the tomb and accompanying relief carvings set into the south wall of the choir – on the evidence of the inscription cut into a panel of its alcove:

> This tomb was prepared by Lord Alexander,
> son of William MacLeod, lord of Dunvegan
> in the year of Our Lord 1528

Alexander does not make his first appearance in the formal historical record until 1498 when a crown grant confirmed him in the lands formerly held by his father under the Lordship of the Isles (which had been forfeited to the Scottish crown five years before). He had almost certainly succeeded his father some seventeen years earlier following William's death at, or shortly after, the battle of Bloody Bay,[2] by which time Alexander would have been known already by his Gaelic cognomen of *Alasdair Crotach*, or 'the humpbacked'. His deformity is said by one traditional account to have been caused by a sword wound suffered in conflict with MacDonalds on Skye and is attributed by another to his back having been broken whilst he was held prisoner in Castle Tioram. Whatever the precise circumstances of his injury, it was inflicted prior to Bloody Bay and would have prevented his taking part in the battle, but it was not to deprive him of many subsequent years of active life noticed by numerous entries in the contemporary records and, perhaps also, reflected in the carvings which surround his tomb.

The figure of a man dressed in plate armour – presumably representing

Alexander himself – lies atop the tomb while behind it an alcove is decorated with carved images of subjects sacred and secular. There is a superbly detailed (and frequently reproduced) galley, a castle which must represent Dunvegan, and the figures of two bishops – one of them holding a skull and identified as Clement, the bishop of Rome martyred at the end of the first century and a popular patron saint in the Norse-influenced Scotland of the Middle Ages. Of greatest importance here, however, is the panel showing a hunting scene: stags startled by two huntsmen, one carrying a crossbow and both leading dogs, who are accompanied by another figure who appears more suitably garbed for war than the chase. He wears a long mail shirt over two longer gowns, one of them reaching to the ankle, an unusually tall helmet of the bascinet type with a mail aventail around his shoulders, carrying in his right hand a great sword and in his left a long-handled axe.

This impressive character has been variously identified, by one authority simply as 'a knight wearing a pointed helmet and a coat of mail',[3] and by another as Alexander MacLeod himself, his costume 'presumably adopted in this context merely to emphasise his superior status',[4] but neither of these proposals seems to me at all convincing. Not only is the Rodel figure quite unlike any other warrior carving in the West Highlands, but there is just so much about him which corresponds to contemporary descriptions of galloglas. His axe, for example, is much like those shown in the hands of the MacSweeney figures on Goghe's map of 1567, but still more curious is the similarity of his unusual helmet to that worn by the soldier (unmistakably a galloglach) whose full-length portrait decorates the charter granted to the city of Dublin in 1582.

Indeed, had this same carving been found anywhere at all in Ireland, it would surely have been immediately recognised as a most important contemporary representation of a galloglach – yet its Hebridean location and indisputably authentic origin there would seem immediately to discredit any such recognition. 'Galloglas' was an Irish term for an Irish phenomenon and apparently unknown in medieval Scotland, especially in the Western Isles where the Norse were never considered 'foreigners' and the origin of the term would have been quite without meaning . . . but then I was introduced to a passage in *A Description of the Western Islands of Scotland* written by Martin Martin in the late 1690s:

Every Chieftain had a bold Armour-Bearer, whose Business was always to attend the Person of his Master night and day to prevent any Surprise, and this Man was call'd *Galloglach*; he had likewise a double Portion of Meat assign'd him at every Meal. The Measure of Meat usually given him, is call'd to this day *Bieyfir*, that is, a Man's Portion; meaning thereby an extraordinary Man, whose Strength and Courage distinguished him from the common sort.[5]

The paragraph occurs in the section of Martin's book entitled 'The Ancient and Modern Customs of the Inhabitants', where the context clearly indicates a reference to the 'ancient' rather than to the 'modern' late seventeenth century – and yet, of course, 'ancient' is only a relative term.

At which point, it is worth mentioning that Martin Martin had at one time held the post of 'Governor' (by which was meant 'tutor') to the MacLeods of Dunvegan, so it may well have been in that connection that he learned of 'this Man . . . call'd Galloglach' and had taken the custom to be much older and more widespread in the Isles than it actually was. If Martin was referring, however unknowingly, to a practice of less than two hundred years earlier and one associated only with the MacLeods, then his reference would throw some new light on the mail-coated axeman in the carving above Alasdair Crotach's tomb.

There had been plentiful traffic between the Western Isles and Ireland since the thirteenth century when it had first introduced the Hebridean and West Highland mercenary warrior kindreds into Ulster and Connacht. Similarly in the sixteenth century when it developed a new mercenary practice in the form of the redshanks, but the traffic was never restricted to the military sphere, nor did it flow in just the one direction. The custom of the kin-group basis of the learned class was arguably introduced into Gaelic Scotland from Ireland, the MacVurich family of hereditary bards to the Clan Donald Lords of the Isles being the best-known example, and Derick Thomson, a prominent authority on the subject, points to evidence that the MacVurichs 'maintained their links with the Irish bardic schools until the seventeenth century'.[6]

If the subjects of Dürer's famous drawing were in fact galloglas he had encountered in the Low Countries in 1521, it is surely not beyond the bounds of possibility that another of the same Irish military professional class might have found his way – even as a prestigious luxury import – into the service of the house of Dunvegan. When the genealogists claim descent from a branch of the MacLeods of Harris for the MacCabe galloglas kindred, it is very tempting to wonder whether a galloglach of the *Clann Càba* had, in fact, come home to the land of his ancestors and there found a surely unanticipated immortality as part of 'the finest ensemble of medieval sculpture to survive anywhere in the Western Isles'.

NOTES AND REFERENCES

Preface

1. James Lydon, 'The Scottish Soldier in Medieval Ireland', in Simpson (ed.), *The Scottish Soldier Abroad* (1992), p.8.
2. Andrew McKerral, 'West Highland Mercenaries in Ireland', *Scottish Historical Review* XXX (1951), p.3.

Introduction

1. Shakespeare, *Macbeth* Act I, Scene 2.
2. Camden, *Annales rerum Anglicarum et Hibernicorum regnante Elizabetha, ad Annum Salutis 1589*, London 1630; quoted in Maxwell (ed.), *Irish History from Contemporary Sources, 1509–1610* (1923), pp.171–2.
3. I am following here, and elsewhere throughout this book, the guidance offered by G. A. Hayes-McCoy, still unrivalled as the eminent authority on the subject, who took the view in the 1960s that 'it seems time that the unwieldy double plural "gallow-glasses" was dropped. The plural form used most frequently by sixteenth-century English writers was "galloglas".' Hayes-McCoy, *Irish Battles* (1969), p.48. I have also followed his usage of 'galloglach' as the anglicised singular form of the noun.
4. It should be mentioned that the same term *gall* was later applied by the Irish sources to English colonists and conquerors into the sixteenth century, and it was this usage which misled Shakespeare's contemporary Edmund Spenser, who lived for some years in Ireland in the 1580s and 1590s, to imagine the galloglas having been of English origin: 'Footmen they call Galloglasses, the which name doth discover them also to be auntient English, for Gall-ogla signifies a foreign youth'. Spenser, *A View of the Present State of Ireland* (1596); quoted in McKerral, 'West Highland Mercenaries in Ireland', *Scottish Historical Review* XXX (1951), p.11.
5. Hayes-McCoy, *Scots Mercenary Forces in Ireland* (1937), p.18.
6. The *Book of the MacSweeneys* (*Leabhar Chlainne Suibhne*); see note 3 (to 'Kindreds'), p.132 below.
7. *Annals of Connacht* @ 1316 and 1317.
8. All three entries in the *Annals of the Four Masters* @ 1358, 1367, and 1377.
9. See Map A, 'Homelands of the Galloglas', p.viii; see also Genealogy 7, 'Descent of MacDonnell, MacDowell, MacRory, and MacSheehy galloglas kindreds from Somerled of Argyll', p.148 below.
10. McDonald, *The Kingdom of the Isles* (1997), p.126. To which might be added Edward Cowan's incisive comment to the effect that 'Alexander's victory drove the first great nail into the coffin of the western *Gaidhealtachd*'. 'Norwegian Sunset – Scottish Dawn', in Reid (ed.), *Scotland in the Reign of Alexander III* (1990), p.126.
11. 'The History of the MacDonalds' – attributed to the MacVurich family, hereditary bards and historians to the Clan Donald – in the *Book of Clanranald*, MacBain & Kennedy (eds.), *Reliquiae Celticae* II (1894), p.156.

12. To avoid the risk of later confusion as to the naming of prominent kindreds of Gaelic Ulster, it should be explained here that the name *Uí Néill* is generally applied to the descendants of the fifth-century king Niall of the Nine Hostages. The medieval O'Neills (*Úa Néill*) were a branch of the northern Uí Neill, the *Cenél Eoghain* descended from Niall's son Eoghan (commemorated in the place-name of Tyrone), but were named for a later Niall, surnamed *Glúndubh* ('of the Black Knee') and styled High King of Ireland, who was killed in battle in 919. The O'Donnells were of the *Cenél Conaill* branch of the northern Uí Neill, descended from Conall Gulban (for whom Tyrconnell is named), another son of Niall of the Nine Hostages and ancestor of Saint Columba.

13. Simms, *From Kings to Warlords* (1987), p.13.

14. See Map B, 'Ireland of the Galloglas', p.ix.

15. Nicholls, *Gaelic and Gaelicised Ireland in the Middle Ages* (1972), p.17.

16. MacNeill, *Phases of Irish History* (1920), p.323.

17. Lydon, 'The Scottish Soldier in Medieval Ireland', in Simpson (ed.), *The Scottish Soldier Abroad* (1992), p.2. Professor Lydon makes reference also to the views of Robin Frame, 'The Bruces in Ireland', *Irish Historical Studies* XIX (1974).

18. Lydon, 'The Scottish Soldier in Medieval Ireland' (see note 17 above), p.5.

19. *Annals of Connacht, Annals of Ulster* and *Annals of Innisfallen* @ 1318. See also pp. 57 and 63 below.

20. Hayes-McCoy, *Scots Mercenary Forces in Ireland* (1937), p.8.

Kindreds

1. *Annals of Connacht* and *Annals of Loch Cé* @ 1316. The notice of the same battle in the *Annals of Ulster* enters the name as *Mac Ruaidhri n Galloglach* ('MacRory the galloglach').

2. Rich, *A New Description of Ireland* (1610), quoted in Hayes-McCoy, *Scots Mercenary Forces in Ireland* (1937), p.6.

3. The *Book of the MacSweeneys* (*Leabhar Chlainne Suibhne*) was edited for publication in 1920 by Rev. Paul Walsh from the manuscript RIA MS – 24.P.25, also containing poems and religious texts, which identifies its author as *Tadg mac Fithil.* Father Walsh places its date of completion between 1532 and 1544.

4. Dr Simms, for example, finds it 'curious' that the MacSweeney family in Ireland 'is found proudly and improbably linking its genealogy to that of the Uí Neill', in view of their employment by the O'Donnells (usually at odds with the O'Neills) through the later Middle Ages. *From Kings to Warlords* (1987), p.122.

5. Sellar, 'Family Origins in Cowal and Knapdale', *Scottish Studies* XV (1971), particularly pp.25–7. See also Genealogy 1: 'Traditional Descent of the Clan Sween from the kings of Ailech', p.142 below.

6. 'The most noble and most distinguished of the twelve sons of *Donnsleibhe* (Dunsleve). It was he who built *Caislen Suibhne* (Castle Sween) in Scotland.' *Book of the MacSweeneys*. Old genealogies of the Campbells call him *Suibhne Ruadh* ('Sween the Red[-haired]') and identify the mother of Iver, ancestor of the MacIver Campbells, as 'the daughter of a great man called Swineruo, owner of Castle Swine in Knapdaill and Thane of Knapdaill and Glassrie'. J. R. N. MacPhail (ed.), *Highland Papers* II (1916), p.82; Niall D. Campbell, 'MacEwens and MacSweens', *Celtic Review* VII (1911), p.277. Perhaps it should be pointed out here that *Suibhne* is a name of Irish Gaelic origin and not – as has sometimes been suggested – a gaelicisation of the Norse *Svein.* While it does not occur in the Irish sources in its patronymic form (*Mac-*) before 1267, it was current as a given name in Ireland from as early as the sixth century when it is

entered in the *Annals of Ulster* @ 564. A Suibhne, king of Dalaraide in Ulster, was involved in the battle of Mag Rath in 637, and another famous Suibhne was abbot of Iona in the 650s, more than a hundred and forty years before the first appearance of the northmen in the Irish annals.

7. George Henderson, *The Norse Influence on Celtic Scotland* (1910), pp.58–9.

8. The historicity of Mulmurry's O'Connor wife is confirmed by her obituary entered in the *Annals of the Four Masters* at 1269, but the *Book of the MacSweeneys* explains the Irish form of his name – *Maolmuire an Sparain*, 'of the purse' – in a folk-tale of his earlier liaison with a *ben tsidhe* (or 'fairy woman') who gave him 'the famous purse' which would be found to contain a penny and a shilling whenever it was opened.

9. Mulmurry's brother Dugall inherited Skipness castle on the north-eastern shoulder of the Kintyre peninsula, which is called 'his castle of Schypinche' in a Paisley abbey charter of 1261.

10. It should be said that not all historians accept this identification, and there is a school of opinion which claims 'Margrad' to have been a brother of Angus Mor MacDonald. That view is rejected by David Sellar – in 'MacDonald and MacRuari Pedigrees', *West Highland Notes and Queries* XXVIII (1986), p.6 – who firmly identifies 'Margrad' with Murrough MacSween, as also does Geoffrey Barrow in *Kingship and Unity* (1989), p.117, and their view is the one I have followed here.

11. It is difficult to believe that they were not, especially in view of another of his cognomens *Eoin na Láimhe Maithe* ('Eoin of the Good Hand'), which is explained in an unusually detailed account of his fighting skill: 'For no sword or weapon ever drew blood of him. He carried two swords and with equal dexterity he smote every opponent. He made three portions of every man he hit, and he was the last man in Ireland and in Scotland who employed two swords as with two right hands.' *Book of the MacSweeneys.*

12. Simms, *From Kings to Warlords* (1987), p.123. The *Book of the MacSweeneys* does offer a tacit acknowledgement of O'Donnell overlordship in Eoin's time in its story of a battle won by the O'Donnell over the MacSweeneys after Eoin's settlement in Fanad.

13. On the restoration of Aodh, his rival Turlough was banished from Tyrconnell, finding refuge with the O'Neill 'and his kinsmen, the Clan Donald' according to the *Annals of the Four Masters* – which would confirm MacDonnell galloglas already in the service of the O'Neill in Tyrone by 1295. See further, p.45 below.

14 The line of MacSweeney descent from Eoin effectively ends with the death of his son Turlough, although the *Book of the MacSweeneys* does refer to his 'grandson' being known as 'Mac Dunsleve' (*Mac Duinnshléibhe*). This would infer Turlough's having had a son Dunsleve who can probably be identified with 'the heir of the *Clann Suibhne* slain in Breifne [now Co. Cavan and Co. Leitrim]' noticed in the *Annals of the Four Masters* @ 1305. The date fits well enough, as does the further inference of Dunsleve having predeceased his father whilst fighting as a freelance mercenary some distance from Donegal.

15. See Genealogy 2: 'Descent of the MacSweeney galloglas kindreds from Murrough Mear', p.143 below.

16. W. J. Watson (ed.), *Scottish Verse from the Book of the Dean of Lismore* (1937), p.258. Professor Watson refers also to a letter (most recently dated to 1310) written to Edward II by John MacSween who complains of Sir John Menteith with a vast force of men in armed possession of his own lands of Knapdale which the king had given him by letters patent.

17. N. D. Campbell, 'MacEwens and MacSweens', in *Celtic Review* VII (1911), p.279. It should be said that the author of this paper – later the Duke of Argyll – had access to a

wealth of archive material, but would probably not have had any acquaintance with the *Book of the MacSweeneys* which was not yet published at his time of writing.

18. Walsh (ed.), *Book of the MacSweeneys* (1920), p.xxii.

19. Sometimes also called *na tri Tuatha*, or 'the three Tuaths'. Confusion with the Irish term *tuagh* or 'battle-axe' has often led to the interpretation of MacSweeney Tuath as 'MacSweeney of the Axes', a quite erroneous translation but understandable in view of the tools of their trade.

20. *Annals of the Four Masters* and *Annals of Connacht* @ 1359. In both entries the annalist styles him *Eoghan Connachtach* and confusingly so because another Ewen in the same generation but of a different branch of the family was also so-called. I will reserve the *Connachtach* tag for that Ewen because his sept, descended from Murrough Og's brother, was settled in Connacht whence it emerged in the fifteenth century as the MacSweeneys of Banagh.

21. See Genealogy 3: 'Descent of the MacSweeney Fanad', p.144 below.

22. Walsh (ed.), *Book of the MacSweeneys* (1920), pp.xxxvii–xxxviii. See also Genealogy 5: 'Descent of the MacSweeney Banagh', p.146 below. Ewen Connachtach's son, Eoin na Lathaigh, may have been the 'MacSweeney, High Constable of Connacht from the mountain downward' whose death in battle – fighting with the O'Connor Don against the O'Connor Roe and the Burkes of Mayo at Kinnitty in Roscommon – is entered in the *Annals of the Four Masters* @ 1397.

23. See Genealogy 6: 'The Descent of the MacSweeney septs of Connacht, Clanricard and Thomond from Donal na Madhmann', p.147 below.

24. The 'MacWilliam' Burkes of Mayo were a branch of the prominent Anglo-Norman family of *de Burgh*, descended from William Og (d.1270), third son of Richard de Burgh (d.1248) who had conquered the greater part of Connacht. The 'Clanricard' Burkes of Galway were another branch of the same family but descended from the younger son of Richard de Burgh, the Red Earl of Ulster (d.1326). The long-running feud between the Burkes of Mayo and those of Clanricard began in the 1330s, by which time both kindreds had become thoroughly gaelicised Anglo-Irish. The rival kindreds of O'Connor Don and O'Connor Roe emerged out of a succession struggle between descendants of the kings of Connacht in the thirteenth century. Their feud was aggravated by rivalry between the Burke overlords of their territory in Roscommon, the O'Connor Roe being allied with the Burkes of Mayo – and later with the O'Donnells – while the O'Connor Don inclined towards the Clanricard. Although the title O'Connor Sligo first appears in the sixteenth century, the history of the O'Connor chieftains of Sligo dates back to Brian Luignech, a younger son of the high-king Turlough O'Connor (d.1156).

25. Richard Berleth, *The Twilight Lords* (1994), p.202.

26. Hayes-McCoy, *Scots Mercenary Forces in Ireland* (1937), p.34.

27. Macphail (ed.), *Highland Papers* I (1914), p.16. The evidence of this 'History of the MacDonalds' is often less than reliable, but does appear to draw on older Gaelic sources and certainly preserves some material unavailable elsewhere which has been shown to be of genuine historical interest. The attribution to a 'Hugh MacDonald' was made by a nineteenth-century owner of the manuscript, and more recent research has convincingly suggested its author as one of the Beaton family of North Uist, which would correspond to the narrative's slant in favour of the MacDonalds of Sleat and hence my references to 'the Sleat historian' rather than 'Hugh MacDonald'.

28. Macdonald and Macdonald, *The Clan Donald* II (1900), pp.81–3; Hayes-McCoy, *Scots Mercenary Forces in Ireland* (1937), p.26; McKerral, 'West Highland Mercenaries in Ireland', *Scottish Historical Review* XXX (1951), pp.7–8.

29. *Annals of the Four Masters* @ 1299. Similar entries of the same event occur in the *Annals of Ulster*, *Annals of Connacht*, and *Annals of Loch Cé* at the same year.

30. It should be pointed out that the identification is less than conclusive, and some historians follow the authors of *The Clan Donald* II (1900), p.30, in identifying the Alexander MacDonald slain in 1299 with Alexander Og's uncle and namesake Alexander (*Alastair Mor*) whose descendants are also found as galloglas in Ireland, where they are first noticed by the annalist at 1367 under the name MacSheehy.

31. Principally the late fourteenth-century *Book of Ballymote*, the early fifteenth-century *Book of Lecan*, and 'MS 1467' (the fifteenth-century collection of Highland genealogies formerly known as the 'MS. of 1450').

32. 'Angus Og, son of Angus Mor . . . married the daughter of Cuinnbuighe O'Cathan.' 'The [MacVurich] History of the MacDonalds', in the *Book of Clanranald*, MacBain & Kennedy (eds.), *Reliquiae Celticae* II (1894), p.159.

33. R. A. McDonald, *The Kingdom of the Isles* (1997), pp. 129–30, making reference to Sean Duffy, 'The Bruce brothers and the Irish Sea world', *Cambridge Medieval Celtic Studies* XXI (1991), pp.68–9.

34. Macdonald and Macdonald, *The Clan Donald* II (1900), p.88. The authors refer also to the MS 1467 which styles 'constables of Ulster . . . under the O'Neill' as the *Clann Eoin Duibh*.

35. Slightly variant forms of the same story are entered in the *Annals of the Four Masters* and *Annals of Loch Cé* at the same year, as is a very confused version in the *Annals of Clonmacnoise*.

36. This Ranald is included in the list of the sons of Alexander Og in MS 1467, but the annalists' reference to him as 'the heir to Clann Alexander' is interesting if the MacAlisters of Kintyre are meant, because that would indicate their having been named for Alexander Og when – as David Sellar has observed – 'MacDonald historians usually regard Alexander, brother of Angus Mor, as the eponym of the MacAlisters of Kintyre. However, it seems at least as likely that their eponym was Alexander Og, the son of Angus Mor'. 'MacDonald and MacRuari Pedigrees in MS 1467', *West Highland Notes and Queries* XXVIII (1986), p.6.

37. See Genealogy 8: 'Descent of the MacDonnell Galloglas of Tyrone', p.149 below.

38. The marital history of John of Islay left its own legacy of complication for the subsequent history of the Clan Donald and has sufficient bearing on the galloglas kindreds to be worth a brief summary here. John of Islay, son of Angus Og, followed his father as the head of the Clan Donald and adopted the formal style of 'Lord of the Isles' in the 1350s. In 1337 he married Amy MacRuari, the mother of his son Ranald (eponym of the Clanranald MacDonalds), but the marriage was annulled in 1350, enabling John to take as his second wife Margaret, daughter of Robert the Steward (later King Robert II of Scotland), who bore him two sons: Donald of Harlaw (so called after his battle fought there in 1411), who succeeded his father as Lord of the Isles, and the John Mor who is of immediate interest here.

39. Latin text and translation of John Mor's letter in Edmund Curtis, *Richard II in Ireland* (1927), pp.87–8, 175–6.

40. K. A. Steer & J. W. M. Bannerman, *Late Medieval Monumental Sculpture in the West Highlands* (1977), p.162.

41. J. Michael Hill's *Fire and Sword* (1993) is the most recent – and readable – history of the Clan Iain Mor I have found. It should also be said that there are two other MacDonnell families in Ireland – one of Clankelly in Fermanagh and another, a branch of the O'Briens, in Thomond – who were neither galloglas nor of any Scottish origin.

42. A 'battle' (*corrughadh*) of galloglas was the customary reference to a formation – supposedly numbering a hundred warriors, but usually rather fewer – under a constable's command. See pp.82–3 below.

43. Professor Hayes-McCoy makes the interesting observation that 'the Earls of Kildare seem to have been somewhat later than their southern relations [the Fitzgerald earls of Desmond] in adopting the [galloglas] system. The first evidences we have of their employing gallóglaigh have to do with a non-Hebridean named Barrett, who, having been driven out of Connacht for some reason, came to Kildare with twenty-four fighting-men at the end of the fifteenth century. This force soon increased to a hundred and twenty men, and the descendants of Barrett remained as gallóglaigh in Kildare until the latter part of the following century'. *Scots Mercenary Forces in Ireland* (1937), p.36.

44. Lydon, 'The Scottish Soldier in Medieval Ireland', in Simpson (ed.), *The Scottish Soldier Abroad* (1992), p.11.

45. For 'coyne and livery', see pp.105–6 below.

46. Such an agreement would correspond to the policy of 'surrender and regrant' initiated under Henry VIII and continued under his successor Tudor monarchs, whereby Irish lords 'surrendered' their territories to the Crown and then accepted them back under terms of submission. These often included a form of title, usually that of 'Earl', although 'Constable of Her Majesty's Galloglas' would have been most suitable for the MacDonnell of Tynekille. It should be added that the specified twelve galloglas to be maintained by Colla and his son are most realistically recognised as a minimum requirement. There would certainly have been a greater force – at least one full 'battle' of galloglas with their attendants and supporting kern – under his command as Constable of Her Majesty's Galloglas.

47. Duald MacFirbis' genealogies descend four principal sixteenth-century septs of the Clan Donnell in Mayo (those of Tirawley at Rathlacken, of Magh Uladh at Aghelaharde, of Coogue in Costello, and of Sliocht Donough Ruadh at Clooneen and elsewhere) from a *Feradhach* whom he identifies as 'son of Turlough, son of Marcus' descended from a Donald, 'son of Angus Og, son of Angus Mor' MacDonald. Angus Og had no known son named Donald, so MacFirbis' line of descent is immediately suspect. If he is correct in identifying Feradhach's father as Turlough, son of Marcus, then the likelihood is of this Turlough having stayed in Connacht when his father and brother moved on to Leinster. The septs named would thus be ultimately descended – as were the other branches of MacDonnell galloglas – from Alexander Og, whom MacFirbis does identify (although by a dubious line of descent) as the ancestor of another Mayo sept, that of Tireragh. These genealogies are set out with additions by H. T. Knox, *History of the County of Mayo* (1908), pp.390–2.

48. Sellar, 'MacDonald and MacRuari Pedigrees in MS 1467', *West Highland Notes and Queries* XXVIII (1986), p.6. I have been unable to find any convincing translation of the by-name *Siothach an Dornan*.

49. Hayes-McCoy, *Scots Mercenary Forces in Ireland* (1937), p.35.

50. Steer & Bannerman, *Late Medieval Monumental Sculpture in the West Highlands* (1977), pp.126 (n.25), 203; Sellar, 'MacDonald and MacRuari Pedigrees in MS 1467', *West Highland Notes and Queries* XXVIII (1986), p.14 (n.24).

51. Indeed, Professor Hayes-McCoy described Connacht as 'a kind of happy hunting ground for all, MacSweeneys, MacSheehys, MacDonalds, as well as MacDowells and MacRorys being leaders of gallóglaigh there from time to time'. *Scots Mercenary Forces in Ireland* (1937), p.35.

52. MS. *Pedigree of the Geraldines* quoted by Hayes-McCoy, *Scots Mercenary Forces in Ireland* (1937), p.36.

53. O'Donovan (ed.), *Annals of the Four Masters*, note 'h' @ the year 1600.

54. Berleth, *The Twilight Lords* (1994), p.193.

55. *Annals of Connacht* and *Annals of Loch Cé* @ 1259, see p.8 above.

56. McDonald, *The Kingdom of the Isles* (1997), p.118.

57. Lydon, 'The Scottish Soldier in Medieval Ireland', in Simpson (ed.), *The Scottish Soldier Abroad* (1992), p.7.

58. Macdonald and Macdonald, *The Clan Donald* I (1896), p.87.

59. Hayes-McCoy, *Scots Mercenary Forces in Ireland* (1937), p.35. It should be mentioned that while the Clan Ruari disappears from history under that name on the marriage of the sole surviving heiress to the MacDonald Lord of the Isles, Amy MacRuari was put aside by John of Islay to facilitate his second marriage to Margaret Stewart in 1350. The line of Ruari does reappear in the next generation when Amy's eldest son Ranald becomes the eponym of the Clanranald MacDonalds, whose territories approximate to some extent of the former MacRuari lordship.

60. MacNeill, *Phases of Irish History* (1920), p.335.

61. *Annals of Connacht* @ 1247; also entered in the *Annals of Loch Cé* and *Annals of Clonmacnoise* at the same year.

62. McDonald, *The Kingdom of the Isles* (1997), pp.175–80.

63. *Annals of Connacht, Annals of the Four Masters*, and *Annals of Ulster* @ 1377.

64. Gaelic text and English translation in W. F. Skene, *Celtic Scotland* III (1880), pp.470–1.

65. Woulfe, *Irish Names and Surnames* (1969), p.324.

66. O'Donovan, 'The Fomorians and Lochlanns: Pedigrees of MacCabe of Ireland and MacLeod of Scotland', *Ulster Journal of Archaeology* IX (1861–2), pp.94–105. Here as elsewhere O'Donovan mistranslates *Arann* as 'of Arran'. There were no MacLeods of Arran, so *Arann* – which appears in the Fermanagh genealogies as *na hAruinne* – is assuredly a further corruption of *na-Hearadh*, the Scottish Gaelic form of the MacLeod territory of Harris in the Western Isles. For the Irish text of the MacCabe pedigrees from the Fermanagh genealogies, see Ua Cadhla (ed.), *Analecta Hibernica* III (1931), p.113.

67. David Sellar, 'The Ancestry of the MacLeods Reconsidered', *Transactions of the Gaelic Society of Inverness* LX (1997–8), especially p.253.

68. If 'Constantine' is an invention, then the cogomen *Caomh* – meaning 'the kindly' or 'the beloved' – might be similarly recognised as a device to contrive an origin for the nickname *Cába*. If *Innsi Breatan* can be taken for a gaelicisation of the 'isles of Britain', it would correspond with the term used elsewhere in the annals to identify the Outer Hebrides and thus lend further support to the MacCabes' descent from the MacLeods.

69 Marsden, *Somerled and the emergence of Gaelic Scotland* (2000), pp.25–6.

70. Entered also in the *Annals of Connacht* and in the *Fragmentary Annals* of Duald MacFirbis, both of which notice the number of axe-bearing galloglas in the funeral cortège, thus indicating the exceptional character of the occasion and presumably reflecting the eminence of the deceased.

71. Simms, *From Kings to Warlords* (1987), p.94. The obituary of Maine MacCabe is similarly entered in the *Annals of Ulster* @ 1455.

72. The Clan Donald claims ultimate descent through Gothfrith mac Fergus from Colla Uais of the Airgialla, and the MacVurich history of the MacDonalds tells of Somerled's having been in exile in Fermanagh before returning to reclaim his patrimony in Argyll. MacBain and Kennedy (eds.), *Book of Clanranald*, in *Reliquiae Celticae* II (1894), pp.152–5.

Warriors

1. Quoted in Maxwell, *Irish History from Contemporary Sources* (1923), p.220. The 'other sort' of foot-soldiers to whom Sentleger refers were kern, for which see p.86 below.
2. Dymmok, *A Treatise of Ireland* (1600); quoted in Maxwell, *Irish History from Contemporary Sources* (1923), p.221.
3. Spenser, *A View of the Present State of Ireland* (1596); quoted in McKerral, 'West Highland Mercenaries in Ireland', *Scottish Historical Review* XXX (1951), p.11.
4. Rich, *A New Description of Ireland* (1610); quoted in Hayes-McCoy, 'The Gallóglach Axe', *Journal of the Galway Archaeological and Historical Society* XVII (1937), p.106.
5. Both Rich and Stanley are quoted by Richard Berleth in his account of the battle of Monasternenagh, *The Twilight Lords* (1978), p.106.
6. Stanyhurst, *De Rebus In Hibernia Gestis* (1584); quoted in Hayes-McCoy, 'The Gallóglach Axe' (see note 4 above), pp.102–3, 105.
7. Quoted in Lydon, 'The Scottish Soldier in Medieval Ireland', in Simpson (ed.), *The Scottish Soldier Abroad* (1992), p.12.
8. McKerral, 'West Highland Mercenaries in Ireland', *Scottish Historical Review* XXX (1951), p.12.
9. A dictionary definition which might have some bearing on the suggested origin of the name MacCabe, see p.72 above. Another anglicisation of *sparr* is sometimes found as 'sparth'. It should also be mentioned that the Irish word for an axe is *tuagh*, so *sparr* can be taken as a specific reference to the pole handle which distinguished the galloglach weapon.
10. Quoted in Hayes-McCoy, *Scots Mercenary Forces in Ireland* (1937), p.61.
11. Simms, *From Kings to Warlords* (1987), pp.117–8.
12. See note 1 above.
13. Gerald of Wales, *The History and Topography of Ireland* (trs. O'Meara, 1982, p.101).
14. Dymmok, *A Treatise of Ireland* (1600); quoted in Maxwell, *Irish History from Contemporary Sources* (1923), pp.221–2.
15. Stanyhurst, in Holinshed's *Chronicle*, quoted in Simms, *From Kings to Warlords* (1987), p.121. Spenser's *View of the State of Ireland* (1596) made a very similar comparison of kern to 'rake-hell horseboys, growing up in knavery and villainy'.
16. See note 13 above.
17. Caldwell, 'Some Notes on Scottish Axes and Long Shafted Weapons', in Caldwell (ed.), *Scottish Weapons and Fortifications* (1981), pp.259–60.
18. Anderson (ed.), *Early Sources of Scottish History* II (1990), p.630.
19. Barbour, *The Bruce* (trs. Duncan, 1997, pp.112–3).
20. The 'quilted jack' – as it is called in Spenser's description of a galloglach – was a linen jacket padded with tow, sometimes also lined with leather or metal plates.
21. 'In tyme past they [the Irish] had no weapons but darts and galliglasses' (1581); quoted in Mackenzie, *The Highlands and Isles of Scotland* (1949), p.154.
22. Hayes-McCoy, 'The Gallóglach Axe', *Journal of the Galway Archaeological and Historical Society* XVII, p.121. This paper contains a more detailed account of the weapon than is attempted here, as also – but from a somewhat different perspective – does David Caldwell's more recent 'Some Notes on Scottish Axes and Long Shafted Weapons', for which see note 17 above.
23. Sir John Duncan, Attorney-General of Ireland, writing to the Earl of Salisbury in 1607; quoted in Maxwell, *Irish History from Contemporary Sources* (1923), p.324.
24. Gainsford, *The Glory of England* (1618); quoted in Quinn, *The Elizabethans and the Irish* (1966), p.101. Gainsford had served as a soldier in Ireland, fighting against Hugh O'Neill's rising and taking part in the great battle of Kinsale in 1601.

25. Newark, *Celtic Warriors* (1986), p.124.

26. Hayes-McCoy, *Scots Mercenary Forces in Ireland* (1937), p.111.

27. As note 26 above.

28. Simms, *From Kings to Warlords* (1987), p.121.

29. Perrot in a letter of 1571; quoted in Hayes-McCoy, *Scots Mercenary Forces in Ireland* (1937), p.44.

30. Hayes-McCoy, *Scots Mercenary Forces in Ireland* (1937), p.8.

31. Interestingly, Professor Lydon has found evidence suggesting galloglas in Munster almost a hundred years before those first MacSheehys in a reference from the Geraldine papers to a 'Gregory Mac Ryry' – whom he identifies as the same MacRory who was constable of galloglas to Turlough O'Connor in Connacht – at the head of a company joining the *rúta* of the first Earl of Desmond in 1328. Although undoubtedly an isolated freelance enterprise, it is remarkable to find one of that kindred so far south and especially at so early a date. 'The Scottish Soldier in Medieval Ireland', in Simpson (ed.), *The Scottish Soldier Abroad* (1992), p.10.

32. *Leabhar Cloinne Aodha Buidhe.* Curiously the galloglas to which the claim refers were those of a *Mag Buirrche*, a name usually associated with the MacSweeneys, who at that time, of course, still followed 'the Scottish habit . . . [whereby] they might serve whomsoever they wished'. See Simms, *From Kings to Warlords* (1987), p.122.

33. As set out in the *Book of the MacSweeneys.* It should be explained that *buannacht bona* – anglicised to 'bonaght bonny' – is variously understood to have meant the actual billeting of the lord's mercenaries on his people or, in other cases, a levy made upon them for the maintenance of such troops. The later form of *buannacht beg* ('little bonaght') apparently represented a general tax based on land values for support of such soldiery. 'Coshery' (from the Irish *coisir* or 'feasting') is described by Dymmok as a later, but apparently similar, form of *coinmeadh*. The text of Dymmok's account of the maintenance of mercenaries (from his *Treatise* of 1600) is quoted in Maxwell, *Irish History from Contemporary Sources* (1923), pp.328–9.

34. A manuscript document bearing on the Ards of Ulster in 1572; rendered into modern spelling from the original text reprinted in Hill, *The MacDonnells of Antrim* (1873), Appendix, p.405.

35. Hayes-McCoy, *Irish Battles* (1969), p.53.

36. Connolly (ed.), *The Oxford Companion to Irish History* (1998), p.291.

37. Hayes-McCoy, *Irish Battles* (1969), p.62.

38. Quotations from the *Book of Howth* are rendered into modern spelling from the original text published in Bryan, *Gerald Fitzgerald, The Great Earl of Kildare* (1933), pp.241–9.

39. Extracts from Ware's account of the battle quoted in Bryan, *Gerald Fitzgerald, The Great Earl of Kildare* (1933), p.249.

40. Quoted in Knox, *History of the County of Mayo* (1908), p.183.

41. Sir John Dowdall writing to Lord Burghley in 1596; quoted in Hayes-McCoy, *Scots Mercenary Forces in Ireland* (1937), p.75.

42. See note 24 above.

Perpectives and Parallels

1. The bard Teige Og O'Huiginn's address to Niall Og O'Neill (inaugurated in 1397); quoted in Hayes-McCoy, *Scots Mercenary Forces in Ireland* (1937), p.24.

2. R. A. McDonald, *The Kingdom of the Isles* (1997), p.66.

3. *Annals of Tigernach* (continuation) @ 1164.

4. John Bannerman, *Studies in the History of Dalriada* (1974), pp.152–4.

5. Campbell, *A History of Clan Campbell* I (2000), p.194.

6. Simms, *From Kings to Warlords* (1987), p.117. It was at one time thought that Ireland did have its own 'mercenary tradition' some six hundred years before the Scandinavian impact, a belief based upon the bands of hunter-warriors called *fiana* associated with the mythical hero *Finn mac Cumhaill* in an Irish folk tradition already known in eighth-century texts. Professor Hayes-McCoy, for example, suggested – in his *Scots Mercenary Forces* (1937), p.25 – that 'the position of the Fiana approximated in some degree to that held by the great mercenary families of the MacDonalds, MacSweeneys and MacSheehys', but that view would be shared by few, if any, modern Irish historians. Dr Simms (p.116) points to the most recent research which has identified the *fiana* as 'devotees of a pagan warrior cult' rather than a permanent military force.

7. George Henderson, *The Norse Influence on Celtic Scotland* (1910), p.118.

8. Stanyhurst, *De Rebus in Hibernia Gestis* (1584); quoted in McKerral, 'West Highland Mercenaries in Ireland', *Scottish Historical Review* XXX (1951), p.10.

9. Magnusson & Pálsson (eds.), *King Harald's Saga* (1966), p.31.

10. Davidson, *The Viking Road to Byzantium* (1976), p.232.

11. 'Ketil *Find* with the gall-gaedhil', *Annals of Ulster* @ 857. For Ketil, see A. P. Smyth, *Scandinavian Kings in the British Isles* (1977), pp.118–126. He is known in the Icelandic sources as Ketil *Flatnef* whose daughter Aud migrated to Iceland from Caithness in the later ninth century. From her were descended the Ulf Ospaksson and Bolli Bollasson whose services with the Varangian Guard in the eleventh century are recorded in *King Harald's Saga* (chaps. 9, 14) and *Laxdaela Saga* (chaps. 73, 77) respectively.

Afterword

1. Pringle (ed.), *The Ancient Monuments of the Western Isles* (1994), p.52.

2. The precise date of the battle of Bloody Bay is not known but is usually assigned to c.1481. It was a sea-fight off Mull in which the fleet of John MacDonald, the last Lord of the Isles, and his allies – including the MacLeod of Harris and Dunvegan – were defeated by a galley force led by his own illegitimate son Angus Og. It was his inability to restrain Angus Og's rebellion which eventually led to John's forfeiture of his lordship of the Isles in 1493.

3. See note 1 above.

4. Steer and Bannerman, *Late Medieval Monumental Sculpture in the West Highlands* (1977), p.186.

5. Martin, *A Description of the Western Islands of Scotland*, facsimile of the 1716 edition (1981), p.104.

6. Thomson, *An Introduction to Gaelic Poetry* (1989), p.39.

GENEALOGIES

1. Traditional Descent of the Clan Sween from the kings of Ailech
2. Descent of the MacSweeney galloglas kindreds from Murrough Mear
3. Descent of the MacSweeney Fanad
4. Descent of the MacSweeney Tuath
5. Descent of the MacSweeney Banagh
6. Descent of the MacSweeney septs of Connacht, Clanricard and Thomond from Donal na Madhmann
7. Descent of the MacDonnell, MacDowell, MacRory and MacSheehy galloglas kindreds from Somerled of Argyll
8. Descent of the MacDonnell Galloglas of Tyrone
9. Descent of the MacDonnell Galloglas of Connacht and Leinster
10. Descent of the MacSheehys
11. Descent of the MacDowell Galloglas
12. Descent of the MacCabes from the MacLeods of Harris – according to MacFirbis genealogies

— I —

Traditional Descent of the Clan Sween from the kings of Ailech

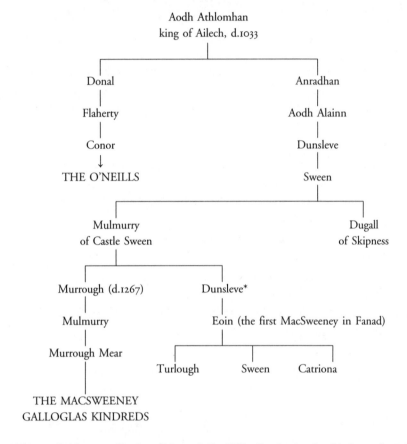

* This son of Mulmurry and brother of Murrough identified as Dunsleve in a Scottish charter of 1262 is taken to be the same person known as Sween in the *Book of the MacSweeneys*.

— 2 —

Descent of the MacSweeney galloglas kindreds from Murrough Mear

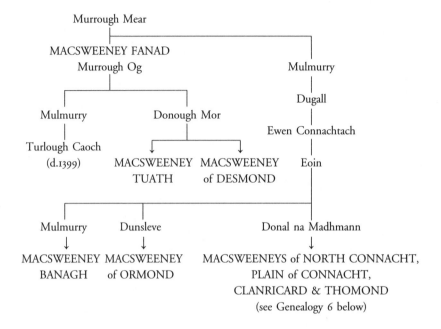

— 3 —

Descent of the MacSweeney Fanad

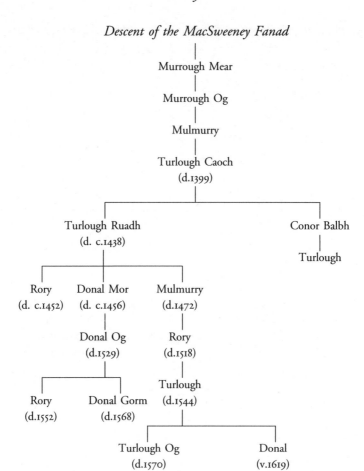

Murrough Mear

Murrough Og

Mulmurry

Turlough Caoch
(d.1399)

Turlough Ruadh
(d. c.1438)

Conor Balbh

Turlough

Rory
(d. c.1452)

Donal Mor
(d. c.1456)

Mulmurry
(d.1472)

Donal Og
(d.1529)

Rory
(d.1518)

Rory
(d.1552)

Donal Gorm
(d.1568)

Turlough
(d.1544)

Turlough Og
(d.1570)

Donal
(v.1619)

— 4 —

Descent of the MacSweeney Tuath

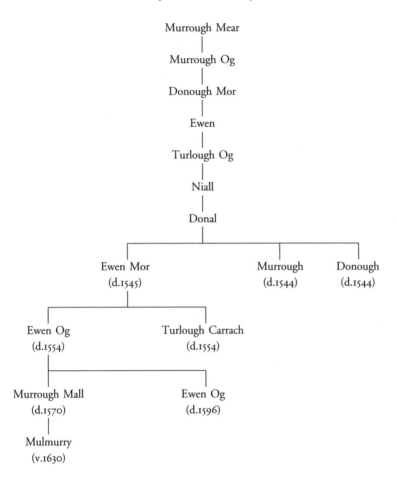

Murrough Mear

Murrough Og

Donough Mor

Ewen

Turlough Og

Niall

Donal

Ewen Mor
(d.1545)

Murrough
(d.1544)

Donough
(d.1544)

Ewen Og
(d.1554)

Turlough Carrach
(d.1554)

Murrough Mall
(d.1570)

Ewen Og
(d.1596)

Mulmurry
(v.1630)

– 5 –

Descent of the MacSweeney Banagh

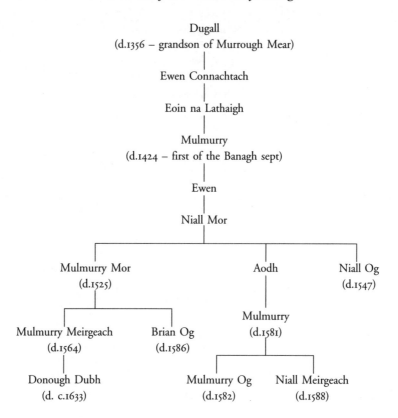

Dugall
(d.1356 – grandson of Murrough Mear)

Ewen Connachtach

Eoin na Lathaigh

Mulmurry
(d.1424 – first of the Banagh sept)

Ewen

Niall Mor

Mulmurry Mor   Aodh   Niall Og
(d.1525)   (d.1547)

Mulmurry
(d.1581)

Mulmurry Meirgeach   Brian Og
(d.1564)   (d.1586)

Donough Dubh   Mulmurry Og   Niall Meirgeach
(d. c.1633)   (d.1582)   (d.1588)

– 6 –

Descent of the MacSweeney septs of
North Connacht, the Plain of Connacht, Clanricard and Thomond
from Donal na Madhmann

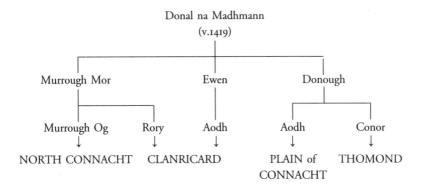

Donal na Madhmann
(v.1419)

Murrough Mor Ewen Donough

Murrough Og Rory Aodh Aodh Conor

NORTH CONNACHT CLANRICARD PLAIN of THOMOND
CONNACHT

– 7 –

Descent of the MacDonnell, MacDowell,
MacRory and MacSheehy galloglas kindreds
from Somerled of Argyll

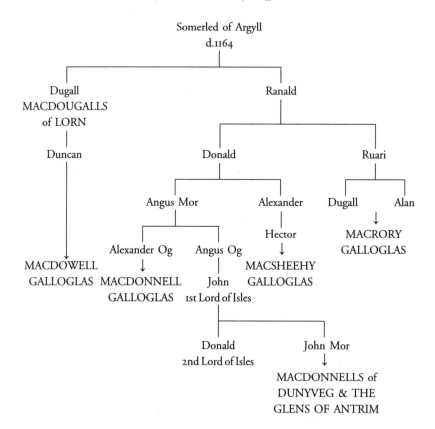

– 8 –

Descent of the MacDonnell Galloglas of Tyrone

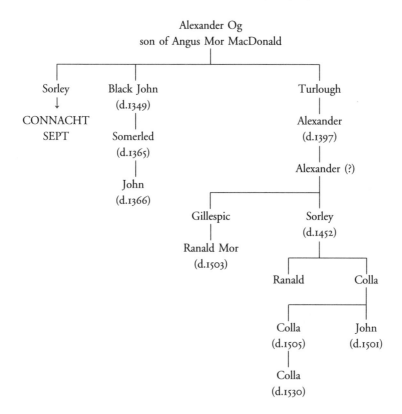

– 9 –

Descent of the MacDonnell Galloglas of Connacht and Leinster

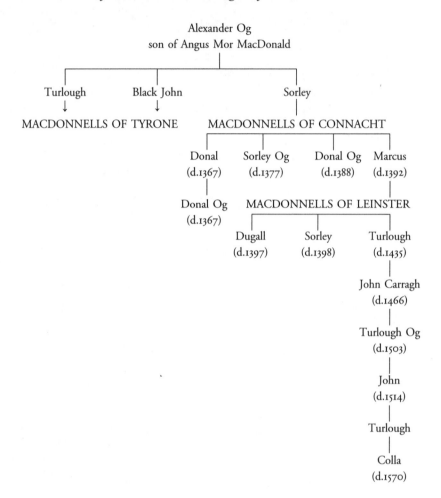

Alexander Og
son of Angus Mor MacDonald

Turlough   Black John   Sorley

MACDONNELLS OF TYRONE   MACDONNELLS OF CONNACHT

Donal   Sorley Og   Donal Og   Marcus
(d.1367)   (d.1377)   (d.1388)   (d.1392)

Donal Og   MACDONNELLS OF LEINSTER
(d.1367)

Dugall   Sorley   Turlough
(d.1397)   (d.1398)   (d.1435)

John Carragh
(d.1466)

Turlough Og
(d.1503)

John
(d.1514)

Turlough

Colla
(d.1570)

— 10 —

Descent of the MacSheehys

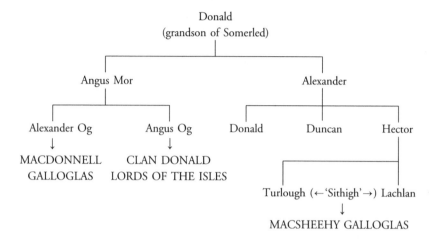

Donald
(grandson of Somerled)

Angus Mor · Alexander

Alexander Og · Angus Og · Donald · Duncan · Hector

↓ MACDONNELL GALLOGLAS

↓ CLAN DONALD LORDS OF THE ISLES

Turlough (←'Sithigh'→) Lachlan
↓
MACSHEEHY GALLOGLAS

— 11 —

Descent of the MacDowell Galloglas
(speculative genealogy based on MS 1467 and Book of Lecan)

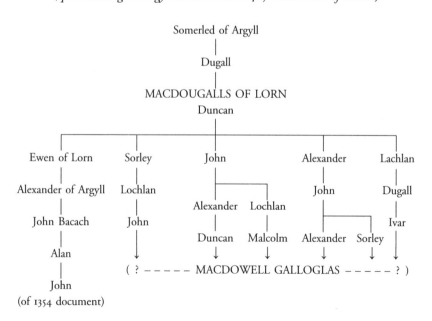

Somerled of Argyll
|
Dugall
|
MACDOUGALLS OF LORN
Duncan

Ewen of Lorn · Sorley · John · Alexander · Lachlan

Alexander of Argyll · Lochlan · · John · Dugall

John Bacach · John · Alexander · Lochlan · · Ivar

Alan · · Duncan · Malcolm · Alexander · Sorley

John
(of 1354 document)

(? – – – – – MACDOWELL GALLOGLAS – – – – – ?)

— 12 —

Descent of the MacCabes
from the MacLeods of Harris
— according to Duald MacFirbis' genealogies

(NB. names in *Italics* also entered in MacLeod pedigree)

Lochlann Leosach
|
Constantine Caomh of Innis Breatan
|
Tormod, 'who was called MacCaba'
|
Alexander [of] Arann
|
Gillachrist
|
Flaherty
|
Gillachrist
|
Enri
(d.1460)
|
Donough
|
Manus
|
Rory

BIBLIOGRAPHY

Anderson, A. O. (ed./trs.), *Early Sources of Scottish History* AD *500–1286*, 2 vols. Edinburgh, 1922; rev. Stamford, 1990

Annals of Clonmacnoise, see under Murphy

Annals of Connacht, see under Freeman

Annals of the Four Masters, see under O'Donovan

Annals of Loch Cé, see under Hennessy

Annals of Ulster, see under Hennessy & MacCarthy

Bannerman, J., *Studies in the History of Dalriada*, Edinburgh, 1974

Barbour, John, see under Duncan

Barrow, G. W. S., *Kingship and Unity: Scotland 1000–1306*, rev. Edinburgh, 1989

Berleth, R., *The Twilight Lords*, New York, 1994

Blöndal, S. (trs. Benedikz, B. S.), *The Varangians of Byzantium*, Cambridge, 1978

Bryan, D., *Gerald Fitzgerald, The Great Earl of Kildare 1456–1513*, Dublin & Cork, 1933

Caldwell, D. H., 'Some Notes on Scottish Axes and Long Shafted Weapons' in Caldwell (ed.), *Scottish Weapons & Fortifications 1100–1800*, Edinburgh, 1981

Campbell, A., *A History of Clan Campbell* I, Edinburgh, 2000

Campbell, N. D., 'MacEwens and MacSweens', *Celtic Review* VII, 1911

Clanranald, Book of, see under MacBain & Kennedy; see also Skene, *Celtic Scotland* III

Connolly, S. J. (ed.), *The Oxford Companion to Irish History*, Oxford, 1998

Cowan, E. J., 'Norwegian Sunset – Scottish Dawn: Hakon IV and Alexander III', in Reid (ed.) *Scotland in the Reign of Alexander III*, 1990

Davidson, H. R. E., *The Viking Road to Byzantium*, London, 1976

Donaldson, G., *A Northern Commonwealth – Scotland and Norway*, Edinburgh, 1990

Duncan, A. A. M. (ed./trs.), *John Barbour: The Bruce*, Edinburgh, 1997

— and Brown, A. L., 'Argyll and the Isles in the earlier Middle Ages', *Proceedings of the Society of Antiquaries of Scotland* XC, 1956–7

Edwards, R. D., *An Atlas of Irish History*, London, 1981

Foote, P. G. and Wilson, D. M., *The Viking Achievement*, London, 1980

Freeman, A. M. (ed./trs.), *Annála Connacht: The Annals of Connacht* AD *1224–1544*, Dublin, 1944

Gerald of Wales (*Giraldus Cambrensis*), see under O'Meara

Graham, R. C., *The Carved Stones of Islay*, Glasgow, 1895

Graham-Campbell, J., *A Cultural Atlas of the Viking World*, Oxford, 1994

Hayes-McCoy, G. A., *Scots Mercenary Forces in Ireland 1565–1603*, Dublin & London, 1937

—, 'The Gallóglach Axe', *Journal of the Galway Archaeological and Historical Society* XVII, 1937

—, 'Strategy and Tactics in Irish Warfare 1593–1601', *Irish Historical Studies* II, 1940–41

—, *Irish Battles: A military history of Ireland*, London, 1969

Heath, I., *The Irish Wars 1485–1603*, London, 1993

Henderson, G., *The Norse Influence on Celtic Scotland*, Glasgow, 1910

Hennessy, W. M. (ed./trs.), *The Annals of Loch Cé: a chronicle of Irish affairs from 1014 to 1590*, 2 vols. London, 1871; rep. Dublin 2000

— and MacCarthy, B. (ed./trs.), *The Annals of Ulster: a chronicle of Irish affairs from AD 431 to AD 1540*, 4 vols. Dublin, 1895

Hill, G., *An Historical Account of the MacDonnells of Antrim*, Belfast, 1873

Hill, J. M., *Celtic Warfare 1595–1763*, Edinburgh, 1986

—, *Fire and Sword: Sorley Boy MacDonnell and the Rise of Clan Ian Mor 1538–90*, London 1993

Hunt, J., *Irish Medieval Figure Sculpture 1200–1600*, Dublin & London, 1974

Killanin, Lord & Duignan, M. V. (rev. Harbison, P.), *The Shell Guide to Ireland*, London, 1989

Knox, H. T., *The History of the County of Mayo to the close of the sixteenth century*, Dublin, 1908; rep. 1982

Lamont, W. D., *Ancient and Medieval Sculptured Stones of Islay*, Edinburgh and London, 1968; rep. Glasgow, 1988

—, 'Angus of Islay, son of Angus Mor', *Scottish Historical Review* LX, 1981

Logan, F. D., *The Vikings in History*, London, 1991

Lydon, J., 'The Scottish Soldier in Medieval Ireland: the Bruce invasion and the galloglass', in Simpson (ed.), *The Scottish Soldier Abroad*, 1992

MacBain, A. and Kennedy, J. (ed.), Cameron, A. (trs.), 'The History of the MacDonalds' from the *Books of Clanranald*, *Reliquiae Celticae* II, 1894

Macdonald, A. and A., *The Clan Donald*, 3 vols. Inverness, 1896–1904

MacDonald of Sleat, Hugh, see under Macphail

McDonald, R. A., *The Kingdom of the Isles: Scotland's Western Seaboard, c.1100–c.1336*, East Linton, 1997

Mackenzie, W. C., *The Highlands and Isles of Scotland: An Historical Survey*, rev. Edinburgh, 1949

McKerral, A., 'West Highland Mercenaries in Ireland', *Scottish Historical Review* XXX, 1951

McNamee, C., *The Wars of the Bruces: Scotland, England and Ireland 1306–1328*, East Linton, 1997

MacNeill, E., *Phases of Irish History*, Dublin, 1920

Macphail, J. R. N. (ed.), 'History of the MacDonalds' (attrib. Hugh MacDonald of Sleat), *Highland Papers* I, Edinburgh, 1914

—, 'Ane Accompt of the Genealogie of the Campbells', *Highland Papers* II, Edinburgh, 1916

Magnusson, M. & Pálsson, H. (ed./trs.), *King Harald's Saga*, Harmondsworth, 1966

—, *Laxdaela Saga*, Harmondsworth, 1969

Marsden, J., *Somerled and the emergence of Gaelic Scotland*, East Linton, 2000

Martin, M., *A Description of the Western Islands of Scotland*, (1716 edn. in facsimile) Edinburgh, 1981

Maxwell, C. (ed.), *Irish History from Contemporary Sources 1509–1610*, London, 1923

Murphy, D. (ed.), *The Annals of Clonmacnoise from the earliest period to 1408*, Dublin, 1896; rep. Felinfach, 1993

Newark, T., 'Irish Warlords – Irish Warriors, 1014–1346', *Military Illustrated* 75, 1974

—, '"As if they came from China" – Irish Warriors, 16th century', *Military Illustrated* 76, 1974

—, *Celtic Warriors*, London, 1986

Nicholls, K., *Gaelic and Gaelicised Ireland in the Middle Ages*, Dublin and London, 1972

Nicholson, R., *Scotland: The Later Middle Ages*, Edinburgh, 1974; rep. 1978

O'Domhnaill, S., 'Warfare in sixteenth-century Ireland', *Irish Historical Studies* V, 1944–7

O'Donovan, J. (ed./trs.), *Annala Rioghachta Eireann: Annals of the Kingdom of Ireland by the Four Masters from the earliest period to the year 1616*, 7 vols. Dublin, 1854; rep. New York, 1966

—, 'The Fomorians and Lochlanns: Pedigrees of MacCabe of Ireland and MacLeod of Scotland', *Ulster Journal of Archaeology* IX, 1861–2

O'Meara, J. (trs.), *Gerald of Wales: The History and Topography of Ireland*, London, 1982

Otway-Ruthven, A. T., *A History of Medieval Ireland*, London and New York, 1968

Pringle, D. (ed.), *The Ancient Monuments of the Western Isles*, Edinburgh, 1994

Quinn, D. B., *The Elizabethans and the Irish*, New York, 1966

Reid, N. H. (ed.), *Scotland in the Reign of Alexander III 1249–1286*, Edinburgh, 1990

Rixson, D., *The West Highland Galley*, Edinburgh, 1998

Sellar, W. D. H., 'The Origins and Ancestry of Somerled', *Scottish Historical Review* XLV, 1966

—, 'Family Origins in Cowal and Knapdale', *Scottish Studies* XV, 1971

—, 'The Ancestry of the MacLeods Reconsidered', *Transactions of the Gaelic Society of Inverness* LX, 1997–8

—, 'MacDonald and MacRuari Pedigrees in MS 1467', *West Highland Notes and Queries* XXVIII, 1986

Simms, K., 'Warfare in the medieval Gaelic Lordships', *The Irish Sword* 12, 1975–6

—, *From Kings to Warlords: The Changing Political Structure of Gaelic Ireland in the Later Middle Ages*, Woodbridge, Suffolk, 1987

Simpson, G. G. (ed.), *The Scottish Soldier Abroad 1247–1967*, Edinburgh, 1992

Skene, W. F., *Celtic Scotland – A History of Ancient Alban*, 3 vols. Edinburgh, 1876–80

Smyth, A. P., *Scandinavian Kings in the British Isles 850–880*, Oxford, 1977

Steer, K.A. & Bannerman, J. W. M., *Late Medieval Monumental Sculpture in the West Highlands*, Edinburgh, 1977

Thomson, D., *An Introduction to Gaelic Poetry*, Edinburgh, 1989

Ua Cadhla, C. (ed.), '*Geinealaighe Fearmanach*', *Analecta Hibernica* III, 1931

Walsh, P. (ed./trs.), *Leabhar Chlainne Suibhne – The Book of the MacSweeneys*, Dublin, 1920

Watson, W. J. (ed.), *Scottish Verse from the Book of the Dean of Lismore*, Edinburgh, 1937

Woulfe, P., *Irish Names and Surnames*, Dublin, 1923; rep. Baltimore, 1969

INDEX